SAINT ELIZABETH OF HUNGARY

ST. ELIZABETH OF HUNGARY

Taddeo di Bartolò
By kind permission of
F. M. Perkins. Assisi.

SAINT ELIZABETH OF HUNGARY
A Story of Twenty-four Years

by Nesta de Robeck

THE BRUCE PUBLISHING COMPANY
MILWAUKEE

NIHIL OBSTAT:
John A. Schulien, S.T.D.
Censor librorum

IMPRIMATUR:
✠ Albertus G. Meyer
Archiepiscopus Milwauchiensis

Die 4 Decembris, 1953

Library of Congress Catalog Card Number: 54-7549

PREFACE

THERE are abundant sources to draw on relating to the life of Saint Elizabeth, Landgräfin of Thuringia. All the known ones have been published by German scholars, chief among them Burckhard Mencke, Oswald Holder-Egger in the *Monumenta Germaniae Historica,* Gustav Boerner, Karl Wenck in his critical study of the Reinhardsbrunn Chronicle, and Albert Huyskens in his *Quellenstudien zur Geschichte der heiligen Elisabeth.* It is, therefore, easy to consult the earliest sources on which all subsequent lives are based. Unfortunately the Bollandist *Acta* cease a few days before Elizabeth's feast, November 19.

Montalembert's *Life* remains the classic which for over a century has endeared Elizabeth to generations of readers. Much historical research has been done, however, since his day and we have now earlier documents than those he knew. A translation of the chief of them, taken from Huyskens' text, appears in the appendix of this book. The documents can be classified as follows: The Relation of the Four Handmaidens, the *Dicta Quatuor Ancillarum;* a longer version with a prologue is known as the *Libellus,* and in it the statements of the Handmaidens are rearranged. With the *Dicta* there is the Letter of Master Conrad of Marburg to the Pope, summarizing the salient points in Elizabeth's life; added to it is the *Processus et Ordo Canonisationis,* and the important record of the miracles at the tomb. The original documents are lost, but thirteenth-century copies exist in Munich and Cambrai.

The first *Life* of Saint Elizabeth was that of the Cistercian monk, Caesar of Heisterbach, and this too has been published by Huyskens. The idea originated with Conrad of Marburg who wished a *Life* to appear before the canonization. It was, however, not written till 1237, six years after Elizabeth's death, and though by that time Conrad too was dead, her uncle

Eckbert, Bishop of Bamberg, was still alive, and the Teutonic Order with Elizabeth's brother-in-law as one of its members was actively interested in her cult. The renewed request for the *Life* was conveyed to Caesar by Christian, a fellow Cistercian also of Heisterbach, who had been present at the canonization in Perugia. Christian took with him from Marburg a "little booklet" which Huyskens has identified as having been the *Dicta*, and this, with personal reminiscences of those who had known her, served as the basis for Brother Caesar's work.

Another *Life* by an anonymous Cistercian, also based on the *Dicta*, appeared in 1239.

Meanwhile, soon after the translation of the Landgraf Ludwig's bones to the abbey of Reinhardsbrunn in 1228, his chaplain Berthold, who had been with him on both his journeys to Italy, wrote an account of his life and virtues. Berthold's original text, which Holder-Egger calls the *Gesta Ludovici*, is lost, but we know it indirectly.

Between 1289 and 1299 there seems to have been a general demand for a new life of Saint Elizabeth that would gather together all that was known of her. The task was entrusted to Dietrich of Apolda, a Dominican in the Convent of Erfurt, who had been in the Order forty-two years and therefore may easily have known people who had been in touch with Elizabeth. He took his work seriously and interviewed all survivors in any way connected with her and visited the various monasteries and castles where she had stayed. He declares that he added nothing to what he was told, but we all know how the memories of fifty years can become embellished. He quotes his sources as having been the *Libellus de Dictis Quatuor Ancillarum*, a sermon beginning *"Mulierem Fortem"* by a fellow Dominican, Otho, another sermon *"Ad Decus et Honorem,"* and others whom he enumerates as *Chronica Scripta Diversorum* which must have included the *Gesta Ludovici*.

Dietrich's *Life of Saint Elizabeth* was published by Heinrich Canisius at Ingolstadt in 1604, re-edited by Jacob Basnage in

1725, and again by Huyskens in 1908. It was from him that Montalembert took his facts.

Perhaps it was partly the success of Dietrich von Apolda's life of Elizabeth which made the monks of Reinhardsbrunn anxious for a more complete life of Ludwig written by one of themselves. The author made use of passages from Dietrich's *Life,* of the *Gesta Ludovici,* and probably of traditions handed down in the monastery which had been Ludwig's favorite sanctuary; it also recorded several miracles considered to have happened at his tomb. This new *Life* was translated into German by Friedrich Ködiz von Salfeld in the early fourteenth century, and it was inserted into the Chronicle of Reinhardsbrunn which was written between 1340 and 1349.

Dietrich von Apolda closes the first period of Elizabeth literature; after him a number of authors chiefly in France and Germany embroidered the main themes with legends varying according to time and place. These compositions were both in prose and verse beginning with the Trouvère Rutbeuf, the *Passional,* the *Düringische Chronik* of Johannes Rothe, on into modern times. A number of legends grew up in Franciscan circles, and though it is disappointing to find no mention of Elizabeth in Tommaso di Celano who was in Germany during her lifetime, Wadding in the sixteenth century was able to quote a manuscript in Louvain on her relations with Saint Francis.

The one fact always associated with Saint Elizabeth is the miracle of the roses; in her story it takes the place of the Preaching to the Birds in that of Francis, indeed its poetry cannot fail to delight anyone. Such stories, however, when divorced from their context, tend to limit and therefore to falsify the proportions of sanctity. The saints are witnesses to the reality of Christ's triumph, for they show what human beings can be when they are faithful to the divine grace of baptism and to the call of God. They show the redeemed creature suffering and working with Christ, using His weapons, and with Him conquering the evil of the world. They stand out

as witnesses to Christ's vivifying presence in His Church and to
the fulfillment of God's promises in our midst. These wonderful
human beings cannot be known through any single episodes.

Reading the accounts of Elizabeth left by her contemporaries
tempts each of us to reconstruct her story; yet how far did those
who knew her really penetrate into the mystery of her personality and being? Inevitably the question applies to us far
more than to them! We know certain facts; there are definite
indications which can be linked together; and for the rest
the most we can say is that we may not be completely wrong.
This, at least as far as the outward record is concerned; for
none but a saint can fathom the mystery of sanctity, and our
distance from Elizabeth is that of a tallow dip from the sun.
Yet she reminds us that we all, each in his own degree and
manner, are called to share the sanctity of the saints in heaven.
Personally, I am deeply indebted to the scholars of the period,
especially to Prof. Holder-Egger, and to those who have spe-
cialized in Elizabeth documents, especially to Professors
Huyskens and Wenck, and to the books of Madame Jeanne
Ancelet-Hustache and of Doctor Maria Maresch which are
rich in critical and historical knowledge. I owe special gratitude
to Princess Solms Braunfels and to Fraülein Maria Helmers
who has allowed me to read her unpublished life of the Abbess
Gertrude, Saint Elizabeth's daughter, and has helped me with
her knowledge, her sympathy, and kindness in supplying me
with books and photographs. Father Zaccaria, O.F.M.Conv.,
Librarian of the Assisi City Library, has helped me unfailingly
with his learning and patience in obtaining the loan of books
from other public libraries, and my warm thanks are due to
Frederick Mason Perkins who has very kindly allowed me to
reproduce his beautiful picture of Saint Elizabeth by Taddeo
di Bartolo as the frontispiece to this book.

NESTA DE ROBECK

Assisi, 1951–1953

CONTENTS

SAINT ELIZABETH OF HUNGARY

*What is Sanctity but
the mystery of
Beauty?*

CHAPTER I

THE WORLD OF ELIZABETH

LOWERING clouds, great rivers in spate, terrific storms with bright intervals; such is the picture evoked in my mind by a superficial acquaintance with the early history of those eastern European lands lying between the Alps and the Carpathians, watered by the Danube and its tributaries.

One invasion followed another making a recurring pattern of conquest, then the gradual cutting down of forests, the cultivation of land and tribal organization of life, to be followed up by the struggle of the more or less settled inhabitants not to be ousted by the next wave of invaders. At the best a reluctant "host" had to offer "hospitality" to successful "guests."

The worst were the ugly, merciless Huns and Avars, but there were also Slav, Germanic, and Celtic tribes, all pushing, surging, and self-assertive. One thing is certain, that none of those numberless human beings who were driven hither and thither, marauding, killing, working, marrying, loving each other, and dying had ever heard of the Incarnation, the central point of human history, and the good news of their own redemption.

Some of them must have heard of the Roman Empire which

had its outposts on the fringe of what would later be known as Hungary and Bohemia; a few must have sacked Rome with Alaric and piled the stones of the Busento on his grave; others among the Huns, the Visigoths, and Ostrogoths must have marched with Attila and Ataulf far into southern and western Europe, and even where the Barbarian was victorious he assimilated a great deal from those he conquered. Contacts were established both with the western empire and the Byzantine Empire; traders began to move down rivers and along roads, at least a few folk heard each other's heroic tales and each other's songs. But still the fact remains that neither the Legions nor the later Franks could make the West really safe against barbaric eastern invasions.

Until the ninth century each central European tribe had its own chief, but the impulse toward coalescence appeared when eight among them chose Arpad of the Magyars as their hereditary leader. The pact was sealed by the pagan rite of each chief opening a vein in his arm, and all drinking of the blood collected in one cup. This tribal coalition was able to subdue what we know as Hungary, and from bitter experience the Germans, Lombards, Franks, and Spaniards all learned to fear them. Charlemagne had established the Bavarian Ostmark as a bulwark against them; they were checked by Henry the Fowler, Duke of Saxony, a resourceful soldier, and a few years later in 955 were really defeated by his son Otto who was to become the first German Emperor of the Holy Roman Empire. After the battle of Lech, Geza, the Hungarian descendant of Arpad, realized that the moment had come when the marauding savagery of Asiatic warfare could no longer be self-sufficient.

There was plenty of savagery, too, in the West, and yet it was a triumph for Europe when Geza appealed to the Pope for protection, and agreed to hold his kingdom as a papal fief. It is interesting to remember that just about that time the first leagues for the maintenance of peace were organized by the Council of Poitiers, when Benedict VIII decreed universal

peace and declared that disputes must be settled by law and
not by force, and the council of Elne promulgated the first idea
of the Truce of God. For the moment these plans remained
pious hopes, but they deserve to be recorded, and Geza at any
rate forbade pillaging expeditions, concluded peace with the
German Emperor of the Holy Roman Empire, and authorized
the preaching of Christian missionaries in his domains. The
tribes of eastern Europe had remained pagan even though as
early as A.D. 864 Boris, the Tsar of the Bulgarians, had accepted
the Christian faith from Saints Cyril and Methodius who had
laid the basis of Slavonic Christianity.

Geza himself seems to have been almost prepared to accept
the Christian God, but he is said to have answered the suggestion that he should renounce pagan sacrifices by remarking
that he was sufficiently rich to serve several gods at the same time.

The first all-important step, however, had been taken, and in
the case of Hungary the Christian influence came in from the
West rather than from Byzantium, and was indirectly derived
from the work of that tremendous Englishman, Saint Boniface
of Crediton. It was he who had anointed Pepin king of France
and restored the discipline of the Frankish Church; then,
as Papal Vicar in Germany he became the real founder of the
German Church, anchoring it to Rome, and helped by Anglo-
Saxon monks and nuns he finally converted Thuringia and
Hesse, destroyed the last pagan strongholds, and established
numerous bishoprics and abbeys. The work of Saint Boniface
dovetails into that of Charlemagne and did much to bring
Germany within the Frankish Empire.

The chronicle of Saint Gall shows what an oasis of civilization a great abbey and school could be, and from Fulda, Einsie-
deln, Passau, Brzevnov, and other places preachers set out and
notably those from Bohemia succeeded in converting the Hungarians. It was Saint Adelbert of Prague, a missionary and
martyr, a friend of the Emperor Otto, a great Christian organizer
who baptized Geza's son by the name of Stephen, and on

his father's death this Stephen completed the conversion of his country, and in A.D. 1000 received his crown from Pope Sylvester II. This union of Hungary with the Papal See was of the first importance since it came not long before the Great Schism divided the Eastern from the Western Church. Had it not been for Saint Stephen, Saint Adelbert, and his disciple Saint Astrik, Hungary, bordering as it did on the Byzantine Empire, might well have been lost to the West.

Stephen was wise, pious, and immensely charitable, and his reign was an open triumph for Christian goodness. He built churches and abbeys and to him and Saint Astrik are due the great Benedictine foundations of Pannonhalma and Pecsvarad of which at least some of the monks had come from Rome. These were the men who finally transformed the Magyar Barbarian State into the "Apostolic Kingdom." It is interesting to note that one abbey rose near the birthplace of Saint Martin of Tours, a great apostle of Gaul, who some 500 years earlier had been born on Hungarian soil, the son of a Roman officer serving in the Legion which garrisoned Pannonia.

Like King Alfred of England, Stephen proclaimed the feast of our Lady's Assumption a national holiday, and even during his life his saintliness and services to the Church were so outstanding that the Pope conferred on him the privilege of having a cross carried before him, extending the privilege to his descendants. In all his work Stephen was helped by his wife Gisela, a sister of the Emperor Saint Henry II, whose wife Cunegonde was also a saint as was their son Henry III. It was an age when saints sat on many European thrones while leading a life of penance, for roughly these rulers of Germany and Hungary were contemporaries of Saint Robert of France, of the two English Edwards, of Wenceslaus of Bohemia, of Saint Margaret of Scotland, a kinswoman of Saint Stephen who had been brought up at the Hungarian court. This prevalence of rulers who were saints had immense importance not only for the personal example they set, but because, at least theoretically, the Christian code of morals was recognized as the common law of the land, and this was a foundation stone of European civilization.

Stephen and Gisela saw all their children die except Emeric, an angelic youth generally known as the "Lily of Hungary," and he was killed in a hunting accident in 1031 a few days before his coronation was due to take place. He and his father were canonized together. There is a little treatise entitled Instructions of Saint Stephen to his son Saint Emeric which shows us the ideals of such a man and ruler as Saint Stephen.* Among other things he advises his son to welcome strangers into his kingdom with their various languages and traditions, "for weak and fragile is a kingdom with one language and custom," and he attributes the greatness of the Roman Empire to its freedom from nationalistic prejudice. In his Christian wide-mindedness Saint Stephen had obviously understood the necessity for both variety and unity.

No sooner was Emeric dead than his father's lifework seemed in peril for his successors were ineffectual in keeping any sort of order. Family jealousy and quarrels over the succession paralyzed all authority, and a recrudescence of paganism threatened to destroy churches, murder the clergy, and dissipate the organization of Christianity. Indeed between A.D. 1046 and 1061 pagan risings and Barbarian incursions were a menace to the existence of the kingdom, but they were subdued and Ladislaus I, another saintly, wise, and firm ruler, was able to restore order and even to carry his dominions as far as the Adriatic. His nephew Coloman was noteworthy in that he allowed the Crusading armies under Godfrey de Bouillon to go through Hungary, but Coloman was cruel and revengeful and his son Stephen II was worse. Yet it was he who founded the first Premonstratensian monastery in Hungary only ten years

---

* For this most interesting observation I am indebted to Mr. Christopher Dawson in "Religion and the Rise of Western Culture," p. 137 (Sheed & Ward, 1950).

after Saint Norbert had made the foundation at Prémontré in France before he became archbishop of Magdeburg, and this same Stephen wished to be buried in a monk's habit at the feet of Saint Ladislaus.

Another weak and cruel king was Bela II; nevertheless he brought the French Cistercians to Hungary, giving their monastery the privilege of being directly dependent on Citeaux. The Cistercians and Premonstratensians brought with them not only the Christian faith and ideals, but also the scholarship, the art, and the agricultural skill of France; it is said that the Tokay of Hungary was a product of cuttings from French vines.

Above all, this constant interchange of ideas, of persons, kept the lifeblood of European spirituality flowing through the various countries, each enriching the others and being by them enriched. Italians, French, English, Irish, Spaniards, Germans, all contributed something to building up and maintaining the unity of Christendom.

During this time there was a considerable German influx into Hungary, partly owing to terrible floods in north Germany. The refugees could find no new homes in the German states rent by internal dissensions, and nothing seemed to satisfy the appetite for discord. The German principalities were in a chronic state of war, of shifting ambitions, loyalties, and interests; someone was always ready to contest the imperial succession which went from the Saxons to the Salians and on to the Hohenstaufens. The Emperor had no settled capital and was also involved in the politics of Italy. At one moment he was the loyal subject of the Pope, at another quite the reverse especially when faced with such personalities as Saint Gregory VII or Leo IX, both great statesmen and great reformers. Not all the powerful German bishops were pleased with the papal insistence on the celibacy of the clergy, and besides there was the crucial quarrel between Pope and Emperor over the right of investiture, and even Henry IV's submission at Canossa settled the matter only temporarily.

In the midst of so many conflicting elements Hungary appeared as a port of safety to German refugees and they settled chiefly in Transylvania where they built towns and villages and became busy in land reclamation and in working the mines. Thus they were a valuable economic asset, and another new western influence in the country was the establishment of the Knights Templar together with the Knights of the Teutonic Order and of Saint John. Then, too, another wave of Crusaders passed through Hungary led by Frederick, Duke of Swabia who, as Emperor, was nicknamed Barbarossa, and Otto of Freising, who was with him, said: "They were so numerous that the rivers hardly sufficed for their ships, nor the plains for their armies." King Louis VII of France was with the Crusaders and in 1147 he stood godfather to the son of Geza II with whom he made a pact of friendship.

The next Bela, Bela III, is of special interest to us as having been Elizabeth's grandfather. This fierce and cruel man was a loyal vassal of the papacy and was western in his sympathies. His first wife, Elizabeth's grandmother, was Agnes, sometimes called Anne, the daughter of Constance of France and Rénaud de Chatillon, Prince of Antioch, and she brought a French and also Norman strain into the Hungarian lineage. Bela's second wife was Marguérite of France, the sister of Philippe Auguste and widow of the eldest son of Henry II of England. On the occasion of his marriage the King of Hungary sent an imposing inventory of his private fortune to the French chancery. The list included his ready money obtained from the minting of coins, taxes on salt and various other commodities, and besides this when the court moved all the food was to be provided gratis by the people. The menu for one meal was calculated on the basis of 12 oxen, a profusion of game, 1000 loaves, and 4 barrels of wine. This rather nouveau riche inventory had some far-reaching political results, for it was obviously worth while to be allied to the King of Hungary.

In 1189 the Crusaders reappeared, led by the Emperor

Frederick Barbarossa, who took the overland route leaving Philippe Auguste of France and Richard Coeur de Lion to go by sea. King Bela met Frederick with a retinue of 1000 knights, and splendid banquets were held to celebrate the engagement of his daughter Constance to the Emperor's son. Bela was persuaded to free his own brother Geza who had been in prison for fifteen years, in order that with 2000 Hungarian troops he might join the crusading forces. The King accompanied Frederick and his army to the Hungarian frontier but he went no farther alleging that he could not leave the country on account of internal troubles. Three years later Barbarossa died crossing the river Salif, and of the crusading kings only Richard remained in the field, but though he was able to obtain a three years' truce from Saladin, Jerusalem remained in infidel hands.

At this moment Bela himself took the Cross, and before his death in 1196 he commanded his youngest son Andreas to fulfill his vow, entrusting him with the funds and war material he had prepared. He had taken every possible precaution to ensure a peaceful succession; his elder son Emeric was already crowned and had been appointed regent of Croatia and Dalmatia, while Bela kept Galicia, which he had recently conquered, for his second son Andreas. Notwithstanding all this, as soon as Bela was dead a nine years' strife broke out between the brothers with the chief result of weakening the royal power.

Andreas used every means to supplant Emeric; the money left by Bela for the Crusade was largely spent in buying support for his claim to the crown, and he succeeded in annexing certain parts of Emeric's domains. The brothers were equally extravagant and the treasury suffered. Pope Celestine III and then Innocent III threatened Andreas with excommunication if he did not fulfill his father's vow of the Crusade, but he was too busy fighting with his brother to take any notice, and things were going so badly that he had to seek refuge with Duke Leopold VI of Austria. At that moment peace in Hungary was essential to the Papal plan of another Crusade, especially because the overland route was again being planned for the armies. The Papal Legate persuaded Emeric to take the Cross, but he turned aside to attack Bulgaria and Serbia to the disgust of the other leading Crusaders. The overland route was abandoned, but in order to obtain shipping from the Doge of Venice the Crusaders had to join the Venetians in dislodging the Hungarians from Zara which had thrown off Venetian rule and given its allegiance to Hungary. Zara was subdued, but Emeric seized the opportunity to inform the Pope that he could no longer continue the Crusade although Innocent had sided with him against Venice. Emeric's excuse was that he could go no farther until his young son had been crowned. Again the Pope urged Andreas to fulfill his father's vow, but this counted little against Andreas' disinclination to leave his brother master of the field in Hungary. Had this not been so, perhaps he might have taken part in the sack of Constantinople and the founding of the Christian kingdom of Jerusalem.

Neither brother would give in, fighting continued all through 1203, but on one occasion at least Emeric showed himself the better man of the two. The rival camps were facing each other; Emeric ordered his followers to remain where they were, and he walked alone through the enemy lines: "I see Hungarians; you see your king, which of you dares to shed royal blood?" No one stirred, and Emeric went straight to Andreas' tent, seized him, and took him back to his own camp unopposed while many of Andreas' followers laid down their arms asking for pardon which was granted.

The story may be oversimplified, but there is something in Emeric that suggests Elizabeth, and after all nieces can take after uncles!

Andreas was imprisoned, and his wife Gertrude went back to her home. She belonged to the family of the Andech of Bavarian origin, but Barbarossa had created Berthold IV Duke of Meran with fiefs in Istria. Berthold had a number of children; Agnes married Philippe-Auguste of France, but as his first marriage was not annulled Innocent III never recognized his second, and threatened all France with the Interdict. To prevent this Agnes returned to her father. Gertrude, the second daughter, was a violent, ambitious woman, while Hedwig who married the Duke of Poland died a Cistercian nun and was a saint. The fourth, Mathilde, became a Benedictine nun in the abbey of Kitzingen. There were also several sons, among them Henry who succeeded his father, and Eckbert and Berthold who went into the Church. It was a family of marked contrasts.

Emeric was soon in trouble again with the Pope over his support of the Duke of Bulgaria, but he pleaded his concern over the coronation of his son Ladislas, and Innocent was placated. After many difficulties the boy was crowned on August 26, 1204, and Emeric feeling himself an ill man looked around for any means of ensuring the succession. Could his brother be won over? Above all, could he be trusted? Emeric took the risk and released Andreas, even making him guardian of young Ladislas before he died on November 30 of that same year.

Innocent did what he could to support the widowed Queen Constance, born a princess of Aragon, and her son. He wrote to Andreas warning him to respect the wills of his father and brother and to defend his nephew, while the Hungarian bishops were told to pay homage to Ladislas. Andreas, however, ran true to form; after the struggles of years he was not the man to let the crown escape him, and Gertrude, who had returned from Meran, egged him on. For such a pair Queen Constance was no match; at last she fled with her four-year-old Ladislas to the protection of Duke Leopold of Austria, taking with her the famous crown of Saint Stephen and as much of the royal treasures as she could manage. Andreas promptly threatened Leopold with war if the crown were not immediately returned with Ladislas as hostage. War was only averted through the death of the child; Constance went back to her own people and three years later she married the Emperor Frederick II.

Andreas and Gertrude had reached the goal of their ambition, and his coronation took place on May 29, 1205. They already had a daughter Maria and a son, Bela, and then in 1207 a second daughter, Elizabeth, was born.

The legends clustering round Elizabeth's birth are more poetic though, it seems, less true than the violent and rather sordid family history. Poems and tales tell how in 1206 six Minnesingers gathered at the court of the Landgraf Hermann of Thuringia, among them Wolfram von Eschenbach, Walther von der Vogelweide, and Heinrich von Ofterdingen. These German troubadours were very like their Provencal counterparts; their favorite theme was love, they were servants of "Frau Minne," they were lyric poets, and Wolfram was a famous epic poet of the Arthurian cycle. At this particular contest five of the singers were at pains to extol the virtues and exploits of their most generous patron the Landgraf Hermann. Heinrich unwisely sang the praises of the Duke of Austria whom he compared to the sun, and very nearly paid for this rashness with his life. The protection of the Landgräfin Sophie obtained the respite of a year, and Heinrich was allowed to go to Hungary in order to ask advice of a famous seer and magician Klingsor, being sumptuously entertained by the Duke of Austria on the way.

He stayed so long with Klingsor learning how to escape from the sentence of death, that at the end only one day was left for the journey back to Eisenach and the Wartburg. Klingsor, however, was not a magician for nothing and he and Heinrich reached the little town at the foot of the Wartburg hill a few hours before the year expired. They were sitting, looking up at the stars, and Klingsor, who was renowned as a prophet, having among other things foretold the birth and career of Frederick II, exclaimed: "This very night a daughter has been born to the King of Hungary; she will be called Elizabeth, and will be a saint; she will marry the son of the Landgraf Hermann, and the whole world will glorify her and be glorified by her."

After this the chronicle loses interest in Heinrich, and it was left to Wagner to transform the story in Tannhäuser.

Klingsor might have read a great deal else in those stars of 1207. Emperors, kings, princes, and their troops were fighting each other in almost every corner of Europe and the Middle East. Two hundred years of wars had followed the appeal of Benedict VIII for universal peace and the settling of disputes by arbitration rather than by force; undismayed by lack of response, Urban II in presiding over the Council of Clermont Ferrand had imposed the Truce of God on Christendom by which people might at least hope for a respite from hostilities for six weeks in Advent and Christmastide, and again during fourteen weeks from Quinquagesima to Pentecost, besides a number of feast days. Innocent III repeatedly offered to arbitrate between the Kings of France and England, and not very long before Klingsor's prophecy he had written to Philippe Auguste and Richard Coeur de Lion: "We, the Vicar of Christ must strive for the concord of true peace, because wars bring dire harm on the rulers themselves, on the Church and on the poor of all lands." Very little immediate advantage was gained by these words and efforts, nevertheless something was obtained by the mere fact that the protest was made. Innocent was one of the tremendous personalities of his time; Richard Coeur de Lion had died in 1199, but there were still Philippe Auguste of France and the meteoric young Frederick of Hohenstaufen who was already more than a match for anyone. This youth was to be surprisingly connected both with Elizabeth and her cousin, Agnes of Bohemia, who was two years her senior.

Above all the seer failed to notice the twenty-five-year-old Francesco Bernardone who, in that same year of 1207 heard the Crucifix in the country chapel of San Damiano near Assisi give him the command: "Francis, go and repair My Church which, as thou seest, is falling into ruin." Francis too had dreamed of knighthood, but he threw off riches, pleasures, and family ties to take Lady Poverty as his bride and to lead the life of the Gospel. Soon multitudes everywhere would be eagerly running after him, and his influence was to dominate the lives of both Agnes and Elizabeth.

No prophet foresaw that most salient, indeed unique characteristic of Elizabeth's life which was the pace at which she lived; a pace only comparable to that of the most fleet Arab horse. In twenty-four years she passed through all the major phases of a woman's experience; she was the princess and the pauper; brought up in a palace she chose finally the poorest of dwellings and to tend the lepers; she was the child of the castle, the courted fiancée, the bride, the deeply loved and loving wife, the mother, the widow, and the saint.

CHAPTER II

THE CHILD

THE baby princess lay in her cradle in one of the royal castles of Hungary, probably Pressburg, and no doubt someone commented what a pity that the child was "only another girl." Outside the holiday crowd in their bright clothes sang and danced and feasted her birth, little knowing how right they were! Certainly from the family point of view a girl was less desirable than a prince who could play a more active part in dynastic aggrandizement; still princesses could also be made use of, and John of England, Philippe Auguste of France, the Kings of Aragon and Castille, and especially the German princes were all interested in the news that the King and Queen of Hungary had a second daughter. The question of her marriage came to the fore almost immediately.

Among the German princes Herman I, Landgraf of Thuringia, Prince of Hesse, and Count Palatine of Saxony, was a very important person, partly on account of the geographical position of his territory, and also on account of his own ability. His mother was a half-sister of Frederick Barbarossa; his extremely efficient father had been known as the "Iron Landgraf," and since 1130 the Landgraf represented the Emperor in the

military and civil administration of his domains. At this time
Hermann was a man of about fifty, and the decision of who
should become German Emperor of the Holy Roman Empire
lay very largely with him. He was married twice, first to Sophie,
daughter of Frederick the Count Palatine of Sommerschenburg,
and second with another Sophie, daughter of Otho of Wit-
telsbach, Duke of Bavaria. He had gone on the Crusade of 1197
and sworn allegiance to the baby Frederick of Hohenstaufen
on the death of Emperor Henry VI. The baby was the grandson of Frederick Barbarossa, and therefore related to Hermann,
but political alliances shifted with the wind and the Landgraf
was deeply embroiled in the vortex of rivalries among the
aspirants to the imperial crown.

The chief protagonists at that moment were Philip of Swabia
and Otho of Brunswick. Hermann chose to support Otho who
was also backed by the Danes and by King John of England.
Otokar of Bohemia, on the other hand, supported Philip of
Swabia, and he won over Hermann to whom he was closely
related by marriage, as he was also to the Hungarian royal house.
Bribes were freely offered, accepted, and then not paid. Innocent III, although guardian to the small Frederick, favored the
choice of Otho as Emperor, and Hermann renewed his allegiance to the Duke of Brunswick. Philip was furious and invaded
and devastated Thuringia, assisted by Czech and Hungarian
forces. Arnold of Lübeck relates that they destroyed 16 monasteries, 350 parish churches, and went raping and robbing
through the countryside so that the people were reduced to
incredible misery. At one moment Otho seemed to be winning,
then more Czechs and Hungarians arrived and Hermann had
to surrender to Philip, and was finally given the kiss of peace.
This, too, was not lasting for Philip was assassinated in 1208
possibly by the Duke of Bavaria who was furious when his
engagement to Philip's daughter was broken off. The matrimonial tangles of those years went hand in hand with the
political ones and are almost as impossible to unravel.

At the time of Philip's death Danish troops were on the Elbe and Otho was still being supported by his uncle King John, and by Albert the Great, Bishop of Magdeburg, above all by Innocent III who asked Hermann to revert to his allegiance, which he did. The lot seemed definitely to have fallen on Otho, who set out for Rome to be crowned. During that journey as he passed down the valley of Spoleto Brother Francis, who had recently been converted from riches and worldly ambition to the life of the Gospel, sent the Emperor elect a message warning him of the evanescence of all earthly glory. Otho's imperial dignity was of short duration; he forfeited the Pope's good will by attacking Sicily for which he was excommunicated, and already Innocent III with Philippe Auguste and the German Princes including Hermann, Otokar of Bohemia, the archbishops Siegfried of Mainz and Albert of Magdeburg were supporting Innocent's ward Frederick, the "Boy from Apulia." Philippe Auguste's influence obtained the decision to depose Otho as a heretic and to nominate Frederick as King of the Germans and then as Emperor of the Holy Roman Empire.

At this time the Italian born and bred Frederick was seventeen, handsome and irresistible. Already he held Sicily in a firm hand, and with him a brilliant comet rose on the European horizon. No one and nothing mattered but himself; his ambition, intelligence, talents, and charm were equally balanced by his power to realize his dreams in action. A number of the German princes rallied to him on his arrival, among them Hermann, who may have remembered the oath of allegiance taken some twelve years earlier. He, with others, had changed sides so often in the intervening turmoils that no one paid any attention to it.

The King of France was on excellent terms with the Landgraf of Thuringia whose daughter he had promised to marry, or to indemnify her financially should she turn out unpleasing to him. The only condition was that Hermann should intervene with the Pope in the matter of the dissolution of the King's first marriage, to which incidentally the Curia never agreed.

The ruling families of Europe were all interrelated and the relationships of each one stretched from the Atlantic to the Bosphorus, and in the delicate balancing of alliances a wisely planned marriage could be very helpful. It was at this time that Hermann asked for the hand of Princess of Hungary for his son Ludwig. The idea was probably encouraged by King Otokar of Bohemia, and by Eckbert, the Bishop of Bamberg and brother of Queen Gertrude, who had just spent three years in Hungary. There was much to be gained by strengthening the links between the three adjacent countries; besides, King Andreas passed for being very rich, and the Landgraf Hermann, with his wars and expensive court, had become less so. From the Hungarian point of view an alliance with a great German Prince, cousin of the Emperor, was not to be despised, and already a couple of generations back there had been plans for a marriage between the two houses.

Such roughly is the recorded history of the engagement; was there any foundation for the legend telling how a blind monk had had his sight restored by touching the little princess, and that he had journeyed to Thuringia to tell the story to the Landgraf who thereupon made up his mind as to his future daughter-in-law?

It was a frequent custom of that time that a baby princess affianced to the heir to a kingdom should be brought up with her future husband, so that his home, his people, his language should be hers. As soon, therefore, as an agreement had been reached between the Thuringian and Hungarian families the Landgraf Hermann sent to fetch his son's future bride.

The party was led by the knights Meinhart of Mühlberg and Walther of Vargila who remained to the end one of Elizabeth's stanchest friends. With them was Dame Bertha, widow of Egilolf of Bendeleiben, and a well-equipped and well-armed escort. They probably took the most frequented highway of those parts over the Fichtelgebirge to Prague, and on through

Moravia into the Danube valley till they came to Pressburg where the Hungarian court was in residence. One cannot help wondering what were the feelings of the dark, curly-headed little girl in the midst of the glitter and banquets with which the foreigners were greeted, and when the presents for her were unpacked. Probably Montalembert is right when he says that at four Elizabeth had already given signs of an innate piety, that her first words were a prayer, and her first act, the giving of alms. It is logical to think of her as a precocious child; there are plenty of cases where great spiritual or artistic genius shows itself extremely early, especially when the allotted span of life is short. It is as though the child were subconsciously aware that there is not a moment to waste, and this is the work of grace.

The chronicles are largely taken up enumerating the gifts prepared to be sent to the Landgraf Hermann and his family. Evidently Queen Gertrude took the leading part for the King is hardly mentioned. "Gold and silver" are the leitmotiv of the descriptions, and the Hungarians certainly made an impression of opulence. Rich gifts were prepared for all the Thuringian envoys, and when everything was assembled the original convoy of two wagons was increased to thirteen all filled with treasures of every kind, gold and silver plate, quantities of jewelry, richly embroidered linen and the costliest silken and woolen clothes, coverlets, bed hangings, and furs. To these splendors the Queen added 1000 silver marks, and a silver bath for her daughter's use, with a message to the Landgraf that he should not despise "these small offerings," adding that if God spared her life she would add to them considerably in the future. One account says that among the servants who accompanied the princess was a maid skilled in playing the lute; there were two chaplains, Arkasius and David, and a number of Hungarian soldiers were added to the escort.

Finally when all was ready for the start the Queen presented the Thuringian knights with a silver cradle in which lay the

Princess dressed in silken clothes interwoven with gold and silver. The parting is passed over in silence by the earliest writers, but one likes to believe the assertion of a German biographer who says that the King of Hungary placed his little daughter in Walther of Vargila's arms saying: "To thy honour as a knight I commend my greatest treasure," and Walther answered: "I will protect her and always be faithful to her."

The return journey followed the usual route and it is easy to imagine the convoy jolting along at about twenty-five miles a day and staying the nights in friendly castles, or in monasteries or inns. They met all the traffic of the medieval highway, feudal lords with their armed vassals who were interested to see the Hungarian child-princess, merchants and traders who were certainly interested in the contents of the wagons much boasted of by the Thuringian retainers, traveling ecclesiastics, pilgrims, wandering scholars and minstrels, players, acrobats, animal tamers and fair people to say nothing of all the folk who for their own private reasons had to get from one place to another: all these may well have caught sight of the little girl who was going to be the wife of one of the greatest princes of the day. Who could guess that within twenty-four years of that time the princess would have died in voluntary poverty, and the roads leading to Marburg would be frequented by hundreds of pilgrims going to her shrine to pay homage to the saint, and beg for favors?

In Prague Elizabeth found herself in the palace of her uncle, the King of Bohemia, who had every reason to be satisfied with the consolidation of three important families whose combined lands covered so vital a part of eastern Europe. His daughter, little Agnes, born in 1205 was not there; she had been affianced to Boleslas, son of the Duke of Silesia and of Elizabeth's saintly Aunt Hedwig, and at the age of three had been sent off to be brought up in the Cistercian abbey of Trebnitz. The destiny of both these almost baby cousins was to be very different from what was being planned with such acute diplomacy.

In Prague as in the great monasteries where the party halted there were many beautiful churches and shrines of the Mother of God, and relics of the saints; and Elizabeth heard the story of the holy Duke Wenceslaus who was so charitable that he would carry wood to the poor on his own shoulders at night, who sought out the needy and was the consoler of prisoners. Such was his reverence for the Mass that he personally sowed the wheat and pressed the grapes to provide the bread and wine, and it was said that when he went the round of the churches at night barefoot through the snow his bloodstained footprints warmed the ground. When he offered to fight an enemy single-handed, angels formed his bodyguard, and during a visit to Germany the Emperor saw two angels holding a golden cross above him.

After he had been murdered his blood was still to be seen on the walls of the church. What a story to impress a child like Elizabeth, for whom our Lord must have lived in every crucifix, our Lady in every statue, and for whom the saints were as real as the King and Queen and kind Dame Bertha and Sir Walther of Vargila.

As the cavalcade moved toward and through Thuringia an increasing number of folk pressed to see the child even though they had no friendly feelings toward the Hungarian men-at-arms, for the memory of former invasions and devastation had given Czechs and Hungarians a bad name in Germany. It cannot have been difficult for Dame Bertha to excite her little charge with stories of the castle which was to be her home and of a kind father and mother and brothers and sisters all waiting to love her, and how one day she would marry one of those gallant and beautiful boys. Walther of Vargila sent messengers on ahead and when the princess came within sight of the Wartburg a deputation, perhaps even the Landgraf and Landgräfin with their sons and other members of the family, were there to meet and welcome her. The flags were flying, trumpets sounding, and all Eisenach was making holiday; songs and cheers resounded as the party rode up, and a tired little girl was laid on a great bed of state beside seven-year-old Ludwig as a symbol of the marriage to be.

Meanwhile the wagons were unpacked, and it was said that "no one in Thuringia had ever seen so many beautiful and precious objects as those that the Queen of Hungary had sent with her daughter."

At this time the Wartburg was one of the chief castles of Germany. It had originally been a small fortress built in 1080 by Ludwig der Springer, an ancestor of Hermann, on the top of a steep hill above the little town of Eisenach. A century later when Hesse had been annexed to Thuringia the reigning Landgraf, Ludwig der Fromme, decided that it would be a suitable center to his domains and he employed the architect who was then building the church of Saint Nicholas in Eisenach to enlarge and beautify the Wartburg as the chief dwelling place of the family. The capitals of the columns are the same both in the church and the castle, and were obviously designed by the same artist of the Rhenish-Romanesque school. The former fortress became a spacious building with its chapel, its banqueting hall, its Sängersaal, its state apartments, its Rittersaal, its "kemenate" for the women and children; water was supplied from a well in the courtyard, there were huge cellars, kitchens, abundant rooms for the entertainment of guests, ample stabling, and the castle was a self-contained little world of its own. Despite modernization in the nineteenth century it was still possible a few years ago to reconstruct the feudal life that once hummed within those massive walls.

It was told that the conversion of Ludwig the Iron Landgraf into Ludwig the Pious had come about through what seemed like an accident. He had got lost while hunting, and took shelter with a blacksmith who did not recognize him. He overheard the man abusing the Landgraf for his harshness and cruelty and indifference to the needs of the poor: "he is so base," exclaimed the smith, "each time one mentions him one's mouth needs washing." From that night Ludwig's life took a new turn; the only people for whom he had no pity were those nobles who oppressed their serfs, even harnessing prisoners four by four to the plow. Once, while he was building the castle of Naumburg Frederick Barbarossa came to inspect it, and commented on the lack of battlements. Ludwig replied that he could easily raise them if given three days' time. He sent out word to his vassals and within the three days a mighty encampment arose humming with vassals ready to defend their lord. "The ramparts are built," Ludwig announced, and Barbarossa congratulated him, saying: "I have never seen any so fine."

This Ludwig, of whom we see a reflection in his son and grandson, was also an enthusiast for learning and education, and he wrote to Louis VII of France that he was sending his two young sons to study in the University of Paris. His younger sister Jutta who married Wadislaus of Bohemia was as famous for her learning as for her beauty and the whole family was intellectually gifted. Ludwig III who succeeded his father married Margaret of Cleves, a patroness of poets, among them Heinrich von Veldecke and he was the victim of a nasty practical joke when Ludwig's younger brother Heinrich stole the manuscript of his long poem on the Aeneid. It was Hermann who restored the manuscript to the author when he had become head of the family on his brother's death.

Hermann was a great feudal prince, a warrior and politician and also a keen patron of learning and the arts, in which twelfth-century Germany was very rich. Magnificent romanesque churches and abbeys and secular buildings were arising all over the country, many in Hermann's own lands, sculptors were everywhere at work in churches and castles and palaces, artists in bronze, gold, and silver were producing most beautiful objects, the Saxon and Thuringian school of painting was renowned, and manuscripts in noble script and illustrated with keen imagination came from the monastical scriptoriums, while increasing wealth brought a demand for all the decorative arts. The German drama had already asserted itself, not only in the liturgical dramas which were popular throughout Europe, but also in more individual forms. Some two hundred years earlier the nun Hrosvitha had been busy writing plays in her convent of Gandersheim where her abbess Geberga was the highly cultured niece of Otto I. While German thinkers and theologians such as Gerhoh of Reichersberg were deeply preoccupied with the problem of the balance between Church and State, and the ever present need for reforms, the visions and prophecies of Saint Hildegarde rang in people's ears, and though growing power and money made many unwilling to listen there were others who knew the dangers of the feudal social system. A sense of impending doom made itself felt in such things as the vernacular drama of Anti-Christ which was enacted before German audiences in the latter half of the twelfth century.

All this contributed to the background of Hermann's reign and he was actively involved in every major spiritual and secular question of the day. The perpetual tension between the Papacy and the Empire was continually breaking out in the German lands in the form of bitter quarrels between the great Bishops and Abbots who were immense landowners and practically powerful feudal lords, and the ruling families intensely jealous of their possessions and prerogatives. There can hardly have been a time when Hermann's hands were not full of political difficulties but this did not prevent the artist in him from reveling in the new vernacular poetry that was just coming into fashion. The great romances of chivalry were having enormous success and the poems of the Troubadours and Minnesingers were delighting and exciting, not only the castle folk, but those in the inns and on the roads.

The Wartburg was an ideal meeting place for poets and patrons and every kind of subject was freely discussed. Walther

von der Vogelweide, a thrush of a poet, was also convinced that
Jews and Mohammedans can serve God. If, in a world chiefly
non-Christian, Jews and Mohammedans had to be considered
as finally separated from God, would not the devil claim the
majority, and thus cause God Himself unbearable pain? Besides
his songs of love Walther was quite ready to satirize the abuses
of the clergy and to exclaim "How long will God sleep?"
Wolfram von Eschenbach — a great epic as well as a lyric poet —
held that heathens of noble life are not damned and that it is
sinful to kill a man simply because he has not heard of Christ.
These opinions and speculations give one a clue to the range
of conversation, and besides Walther and Wolfram, Heinrich
von Ofterdingen and Heinrich von Veldecke, many other poets,
singers and tellers of tales used to foregather in the Wartburg,
and with them no doubt jongleurs and musicians and conjurors
and other lesser fry of the profession. Everyone was welcome,
and it was Walther who declared that "if a barrel of good wine
should cost 1000 livres, none of Hermann's guests would have
an empty cup." Evidently there came a time when he preferred
the quiet of his own little property to the boisterous entertain-
ing of the court for he wrote: "Anyone who is of sensitive
hearing had better avoid the court of Thuringia, for if he
goes there he will be deafened. I have taken part in that roister-
ing and I was completely exhausted; night and day one troop
follows another." Guests had to be strong. Hermann delighted
in such gatherings and there were probably many other "con-
tests of song" in the Wartburg besides the famous "Saenger-
krieg." The great Manesse codex of the Minnesinger songs,
now in Heidelberg, is so vividly illustrated that it gives us the
impression of knowing these people personally; we see how
they dressed, how they played and sang, hawked and hunted,
and in those pages the court of Thuringia springs into life,
the court into which came the Hungarian princess.

At the time of her arrival Hermann's daughters by his first
marriage were already married, Jutta, then about thirty, to

Dietrich of Misnia, and Hedwig to Albrecht I of Orlamünde. His first child by his second marriage, Irmentrude, was born about 1196, and therefore in her teens, the two eldest boys were Ludwig and Hermann and there has been discussion which was the first-born. It seems reasonable to suppose that King Andreas would have insisted on his daughter marrying the heir, which would mean that Ludwig was born in 1200, and Hermann a year or so later. There were two smaller boys, Hermann Raspe and Conrad, and Agnes who was Elizabeth's age. To these must be added six other children of the Thuringian nobility who were assigned to Elizabeth as playmates, and especially Guda was her close friend and later recorded most precious details about her. Another intimate friend was Isentrude who joined the household some years later; she and Guda shared all the vicissitudes of Elizabeth's life and also her spiritual orientation.

We see the little Hungarian princess as one of a merry group of children in the ideal playground of the castle with its court-yards, towers, and battlements, and the castle hill so rich in caves and rocks and hiding places. There were old retainers who could tell wonderful tales of Ludwig the Springer who had built the castle, and all the legends connected with it which they had heard from their grandparents; and the children were familiar also with other castles for the court accompanied Hermann when he moved about in order to control the political and economic administration of his dominions. There was also a family palace, the Landgrafenhof, in Eisenach, a place which was fast becoming prosperous doing much trade in wine and beer and cloth.

Hermann seems to have preferred the Wartburg as his residence, and there was nothing circumscribed or narrow about life there with the outside world arriving in frequent, colorful cavalcades and the talk of Europe flowing through its halls. Wolfram von Eschenbach was a constant visitor, and Elizabeth and her companions must often have listened alert and open-

eyed to the feats of King Arthur, of Sir Percival and the
Knights of the Round Table, as well as to the songs of the
Minnesingers. Then there were thrilling tales of the Crusaders
and Christian heroes akin to the martyrs and saints. Had not
Godfrey of Bouillon refused to enter Jerusalem wearing a
royal crown because the Son of God in that place had worn
one of thorns? It may have struck Elizabeth that this was the
reason why kings hung up their crowns above the altar. Had
her own father done so? Had the Landgraf Hermann? Was that
why the old King in the Epiphany play she had seen took off
his crown and laid it at the feet of the Holy Child?

We know how vital a part the imaginative background plays
in any child's life; why not in Elizabeth's?

Hermann with his appreciation of culture was not the man
to tolerate any neglect of education, and according to the
medieval notion children were considered to be out of the
nursery at seven and subjected to a rigid discipline. It was
quite usual for the boys to be sent away, at any rate for a time,
and brought up in another court; what happened to the girls
depended very much on their matrimonial prospects. There is
no proof that Ludwig and Hermann left the Wartburg but like
other future knights they had to be trained according to the
very demanding standards of chivalry. They learned Latin and
possibly French, and it was important that a ruler should become familiar with the intricacies of statecraft, and that his
judgment should be educated to weigh the shifting balance of
alliances and to estimate the personal reaction of the intensely
interrelated princes of Europe. They were encouraged in guess-
ing games to sharpen their wits, and they also played chess
which was a novelty in Europe, brought in by the Crusaders.
Honor, good manners, self-control were demanded of them, for
above all the knight had to be a Christian, and a perfect Chris-
tion at that; such, at least, was the ideal held up before them.

Ludwig and his brothers were brought up on these lines;
they had also to learn the rudiments of the liberal arts, and to

be proficient in physical prowess, perfect riders, good swimmers, archers, expert fighters with sword and lance, able to hurl a javelin, regardless of danger. There was no time to be idle.

The Landgräfin Sophie was equally determined to bring up her prospective daughter-in-law with the greatest care; the first things to be learned were the *Pater* and *Ave*, the *Salve Regina*, and the habitual invocation of medieval German children when they went to bed: "Now that I lie down to sleep twelve angels be with me, two at my head, two at my feet, one at each side, two to cover me, two to wake me, and two to bear me to Paradise." A little feudal princess had to learn some Latin, to read and write, sing, and perhaps play the lute which had also been brought into Europe by the Crusaders; she must be proficient in the different arts of housekeeping, she must know the rudiments of first aid, sew and spin, ride and hawk, and be expert in that other art of good manners and the ways of society. Elizabeth learned all this, but her friend Guda in recalling their childhood lays particular stress on her piety: "She directed all her desires and actions toward God," and this is something far beyond any conventional childish devotion; in all the saints who have died young it seems to have been the hallmark of their early sanctity. Elizabeth could hardly have turned six when she was always on the alert for any excuse to get into the chapel, which drew her like a magnet. During playtime she would artfully manage that even a hopping game or tip-and-run should carry her in that direction so that she might at least be able to kiss the outside walls. When she was able to get inside she would lie at full length before the altar, and the longer she could stay, the happier she was. She used to promise God that should she win the ring game she would make a certain number of genuflections, and if this proved difficult she would suggest that her companions should all lie down so as to measure who was the tallest in order that she should have the chance of kneeling and kissing the ground. She recalled this detail herself in later years. Part of her winnings

— perhaps sweets — always went to poor children, and the only thanks she asked was an *Ave*. This was the example she set her playmates.

Her sense of self-denial was already awake, not only in always looking for something to give away, but also as penance. She would stop playing, dancing, anything she particularly enjoyed "for love of God"; she refused to put on gloves or the richly embroidered oversleeves until after Mass because she could not bear to go to Church dressed up. All through her life she always and unfailingly seized the opportunity for humility or penance offered by each moment; she let nothing slip, and these childish symptoms of what would prove fundamental in her character remind us of Saint Thérèse of Lisieux or Saint Joseph Benedict Cottolengo who, at the age of five, was already measuring his father's room to see how many beds could be fitted in "for poor sick people." Saint Thérèse of Lisieux resembles Saint Elizabeth too in her iron will power; nothing could deflect either of those girls from what they saw as right.

Another characteristic which stands out in Elizabeth's whole life is the balance between her intelligence and will. From childhood she moved among the events of the great world, circumstances brought her face to face with the major problems of Europe as well as with all that was most attractive in feudal society. Her intelligence did not react to any of this theoretically; it served to show her a course of action, and once she had seen the light shining on a particular path Elizabeth never looked back and nothing could force or cajole her into wasting her time or dissipating her energy. The driving power was love.

It was the habit for the children of the court to draw lots for a patron among the Apostles whose names were inscribed on candles heaped together on the altar. Elizabeth had already put herself under the protection of our Blessed Lady, but she also had a very special love for Saint John as personifying purity.

Now for a child what would be the significance of purity if not such closeness to our Lord as to allow Saint John's head to rest on the breast of Jesus? Of course, she was delighted and uplifted when three times running she drew the candle inscribed with Saint John's name. She too must get nearer to Jesus, so near that nothing could separate her from Him; she must give Him all herself, above all things she wanted Him. Elizabeth turned to God with the whole strength of her nature, and this strength had in it the violent temperament of her ancestry as well as the impulse of grace.

In describing Elizabeth's childish devotion Guda makes special mention of a beautiful, illuminated Book of Hours, the work of the best artists of the time. She says that while turning its pages Elizabeth was "lost in prayer," lost in that spiritual world which was so intensely real to the child whose own spiritual life was developing so fast and thrusting down such deep roots.

We must say a word about three Psalters which are said to have belonged to Elizabeth. The one alluded to by Guda is probably that in the Stuttgart city library; it came from the abbey of Reinhardsbrunn, the favorite sanctuary of the Landgraf's family. The book is the work of the Thuringian school of painting, and the scenes are vividly depicted in brilliant colors, and among the figures are those of Hermann and Sophie. Another most beautiful Psalter is commonly known as that of Elizabeth herself; she is said to have given it to her uncle Bishop Berthold of Aquileja, and it is now in Cividale. This book appears to have belonged originally to Sophie and contains portraits of her and Hermann as well as of the kings and queens of Hungary and Bohemia. There is also a medallion of Gregory IX who did not become pope until eleven years after Hermann's death; in the text, however, there is the Landgräfin Sophie's prayer for her husband, apparently written while he was alive. Yet another Psalter in private hands was originally in the abbey of Altenberg and is probably the work of the famous school of illumination of Saint Maximin in Treves.

Looking at these books our eyes rest on something that was precious and inspiring to Elizabeth, probably touched by her hands, sanctified by her prayers; for the moment we feel her beside us.

Many things were happening which had repercussions in the Wartburg. Elizabeth's arrival there had more or less coincided with that of Frederick in Germany, and the following year saw him elected King of the Germans by his adherents among the German princes. Hermann had been at his side for some months when, in December, Frederick received the German crown in Mainz from the hands of Archbishop Siegfried in the presence of representatives of Innocent III and Philippe-Auguste.

Hermann's elder sons may well have been there; all of them must have heard of it and of the new young King, but again no one could have guessed what was to be the connection between the little Hungarian princess and the ruler of Germany. She was to touch him more deeply than he her and in what an unexpected manner.

In that same year, too, something else was happening which surely must have made the deepest impression on Elizabeth's precocious religious sensibility.

More perhaps than anything else the Children's Crusade marks the difference between the medieval outlook and our own. In 1212, the year which saw the German princes gathered in Mainz for the coronation of the handsome, seventeen-year-old Frederick II, a French shepherd lad had a vision in which our Lord told him to go from place to place rousing people to liberate the Holy Places. Very soon he was being followed by a crowd of children who went along singing, and when asked where they were going answered "To God."

Children from the Rhineland also flocked out led by ten-year-old Nicholas of Cologne; it seemed impossible to restrain them, and even when parents locked them up, many managed to escape. They were caught in a wave of enthusiasm, they had been chosen by God, and Nicholas carried a Tau-shaped cross before them asserting that an angel had ordered him to free the Holy Places. In defense of those who must have known the dangers the children were running let it be said that we have no idea of the emotional intensity of excitement that could then be roused in people all over Europe by the cry of "Jerusalem" and "The Cross."

The fact remains that thousands of children set out to conquer the Holy Places with their innocence and prayers; some of them reached Marseilles, and no one appears to have risen in wrath when rascally profiteers offered to convey them to Palestine free of charge "for love of God." In Alexandria the survivors were sold as slaves, except a few who were killed sooner than deny their faith.

Much the same fate awaited those who reached the Adriatic ports, but at least the Archbishop of Brindisi refused to let them go farther. Three years later at the Fourth Lateran Council, Innocent III in his attempts to rouse the European sovereigns to a Crusade, appealed to the example of these children; "they put us to shame for they sacrificed themselves while we slept."

How could such a story fail to impress any child!

The Children's Crusade must have been a burning topic of conversation even if it seemed unimportant to men like Hermann, immersed as he was in the hazards of high politics. After his election as King, Frederick made a journey through the lands of his loyal vassals to accept their homage, and it is not in the least farfetched to think that he and six-year-old Elizabeth may have seen each other; he certainly must have heard of her and of her engagement to Hermann's son, a wise alliance from his point of view since it might be useful diplomatically. He may have looked at her with a certain curiosity, for Innocent III had induced him to marry Constance, the widow of Elizabeth's uncle Emeric. In 1213 Hermann was among the great nobles who assented to the Golden Bull of Eger which guaranteed the rights of the Church in Frederick's German lands, but even in that same year he had to pay a heavy price for the line he had taken.

Frederick's rival Otto had not yet said his last word, and marched an army into unfortunate Thuringia which was again harried and ravaged. Hermann with Otokar of Bohemia joined Frederick's force, but the definite defeat of Otto only came about when Philippe-Auguste defeated the Anglo-Guelph alliance at Bouvines in 1214. After this Frederick was accepted by all the German Princes and recrowned in Aix-la-Chapelle with great pomp in July of 1215. Previously he had spent some weeks in Thuringia, and who knows whether he went to the Wartburg?

Other stirring news had been received there, for Queen Gertrude of Hungary had been murdered in the summer of 1213. She had always been unpopular in her husband's country and her schemes to install her favorite brother, Berthold, as Archbishop of Kalocsa were much resented. A number of Hungarian nobles had never forgiven Andreas and Gertrude for what they considered the usurpation of the throne, and during an absence of the King they assassinated Gertrude though they did not succeed in deposing Andreas, or in catching Berthold, who escaped with a large booty of Hungarian treasure. Whether or not any of the details reached Elizabeth she took in the fact that her mother was dead. The child may have remembered the parting and that silver cradle, and the kisses and injunctions to behave as a princess should. What happened when people died? One prayed that they should go at once to heaven, and it may have been this news that led Elizabeth to take her little friends to the cemetery to pray for the dead: "For the love of Thy dear Mother free these poor souls from pain; by Thy five Wounds save us, O Lord."

Nothing tells us whether Elizabeth thought of her father;

everything makes us suppose that in the gossip of the Wartburg
the question was being asked would King Andreas carry out
Queen Gertrude's promise about a further contribution to the
princess's dowry. Had he the money to do so? It seemed all too
unlikely.

Cloud and sunlight continued to chase each other across the
political horizon; hardly a year passed without fighting in some
part of Hermann's domains. He was still in Frederick's favor,
but the young king had so far failed to reward the Landgraf's
support with certain cities he desired to include in his territory.
There are hints in one chronicle that perhaps Hermann had
been induced to change allegiance once again, and Otto may
have hoped that the game was not entirely lost. In any event
the wily young Frederick could outmatch his vassals in intrigue
as well as subjugate them by the force of his genius and personality, and matters did not reach a decisive point.

On December 31, 1216, the boy Hermann died; he was fifteen
and for the first time the children followed the funeral procession of one of themselves to the monastery of Saint Catherine
in Eisenach founded by the Landgraf and where now they
listened to the chanting of the Requiem.

Was the boy's death a mortal blow to his father? The elder
Hermann appears to have been already a sick and doomed man
who had lost his grip on public affairs and he died on April
25, 1217, three months after his son. Hermann's end is surrounded with mystery, and nothing sure can be deduced from
the vague reports and insinuations of the chronicles. There
must, however, have been some serious trouble for the Landgräfin Sophie to write in her Psalter which is now in Cividale:
"O Jesus, I commend to Thee Thy servant Hermann, for
though he is caught in the mesh of sin and crime, yet Thou
didst create him; Thou didst redeem him with Thy precious
Blood, and he hopes in Thee. Protect him from every evil today
and always; free him from the power, the deceits and traps
and chains of his enemies. Keep him from all bodily harm and

from sudden death. I commend him to Thee in the confident hope that through Thy Passion he may be saved. Hear me, a poor sinner when I pray for Thy brother Hermann." These are the words of a deeply anxious and distressed woman, and the plea that Hermann should not die suddenly gives color to the Archbishop of Mainz's later statement that he was excommunicated though this was denied by Ludwig. The Life of Ludwig written in the Abbey of Reinhardsbrunn only says: "His (Hermann's) virtues, worth and valor were such that his fame surpassed that of any other German Prince, but all praise must be measured in the light of a man's end. No matter how high and noble, the tree lies where it falls. All speak of what is notorious; only God knows what is hidden." In any case Hermann surely died reconciled to the Church for the Cistercians wanted to bury him in their abbey of Reinhardsbrunn but the Landgräfin Sophie answered: "My dear Lord and husband will lie in the church of the monastery of Saint Catherine in Eisenach which he founded, and where, during his lifetime, he expressed the wish to be buried."

Whatever lay behind these ambiguous accounts the atmosphere of the family during those months must have been charged with tense foreboding and gloom, with grief for the loss of the boy and fear for his father. Sophie was a deeply religious woman, with probably great self-control, but her words reveal her state of mind and a sensitive child like Elizabeth must have felt it acutely. This experience surely contributed considerably to her early spiritual maturity. For the first time she came into personal touch with excommunication, which meant a chapel without services, with no Eucharistic presence of our Lord, with the sanctuary lamp extinguished and the bell silent. It brought her up against the frailty of power and riches, into a personal realization of the danger of mortal sin, of hell, and of the necessity of constant prayer. And the sense of sin brings with it the sense of God's mercy through Christ. Who can guess at the work of grace in the mind and heart as well as in the soul of Elizabeth throughout those months of distress? That child who had always been so drawn to prayer must have prayed with a new urgency for those who had taken the place of her parents and with a new realization of spiritual solidarity; the crisis of others was her crisis, a soul might fall into mortal sin because her prayer had been lacking. Thus Elizabeth was being prepared for the next phase of her life.

CHAPTER III

YOUTH

ELIZABETH was ten when Hermann died, and Ludwig seventeen. The Landgräfin Sophie had become the central figure in the picture, and we see her a regal, austere woman, assailed no doubt with worries following her husband's death, anxious to carry on his policy, and estimating Elizabeth's personality and gifts by the formal standards of what was necessary, both from the spiritual and worldly points of view, in the bride of the heir. She was more than ever determined to impose these standards of spiritual outlook, of manners, dress, and behavior.

No one really knows what Elizabeth looked like; we have only a sixteenth-century legend to vouch for her dark beauty. We can imagine her as one of those sensitive and lovely princesses and saints in her niche on the façade of some Gothic church; she is still a child, yet in another two years half of her life will be over.

In considering Elizabeth's story the fundamental importance of the time scale must always be kept in mind. For one thing the ancient and medieval time scale differed from ours, and children came to grips with life much earlier than is customary with us. How many of the early Christian martyrs were very young, and rulers of schoolboy age were mature, for instance, Elizabeth's contemporary Frederick. In her, too, there is the vital consideration of vocation, and the grace of God can always accomplish the completion of a human being in what to ordinary ideas is a very short time. Inevitably we think of that wonderful fourth chapter of the Book of Wisdom culminating in the words: "Being made perfect in a short space, he fulfilled a long time." It is a final description of Elizabeth.

At ten years old the great lines of her personality had already emerged, in Guda's words: "She always most humbly had God before her eyes and invoked Him in all her actions; calling on His Name with tenderness, she referred everything to Him." She was a human being possessed by God, and she knew it; subconsciously she seems to have been aware that she must use every moment, and every opportunity, to express that for her everything was second to God.

Such an opportunity came on the Feast of the Assumption when the Landgräfin announced to Elizabeth and Agnes that she and they would go in state to the high Mass in the church of Our Lady in Eisenach which belonged to the Knights of the Teutonic Order. This meant that she and the princesses would be dressed in the full magnificence of their rich silk and velvet clothes, with long embroidered sleeves and surcoats edged with fur, with magnificent long mantles carried by pages, their gloves sewn with pearls and precious stones, and their persons adorned with golden chains and jewels. The young princesses probably did not wear the customary linen coif but would have had loose veils and coronets on their flowing hair. On entering the packed church they knelt before the crucifix, and then, instead of moving to her place of honor with the others, Elizabeth took off her crown laying it before the cross and remained prostrate on the ground with her face covered.

Naturally everyone stared at their ruler's future bride, and the Landgräfin Sophie called her to order only to receive the answer: "How can I a miserable creature remain wearing a crown of earthly dignity when I see my King Jesus Christ crowned with thorns."

It might have been her own ancestor, Godfrey de Bouillon, speaking. Perhaps the memory of his uncrowned entry into Jerusalem flashed into her mind. Anyhow, the King of Heaven crowned with thorns was more real to her than the Landgräfin at her side. What could be more natural than to take off one's crown in any church, before any crucifix? Why did not all kings follow Godfrey's example? It was impossible to hesitate and she, at all events had to do it; and if her action was not original, she made it into something new and personal and significant by the force of conviction and love that lay behind it.

It was a direct challenge of the cross to the "world"; and for the first time we see Elizabeth deliberately and consciously asserting her own place in the two orders of values. In its own way this gesture was as significant as that of Francis throwing off his clothes, or of Clare who probably in that very year had run away from her feudal home to follow the Franciscan ideal of poverty. We see a child of ten or eleven who dares to challenge the "world" with all it means in the name of a totally different loyalty and love. Elizabeth here shows the same single-minded purpose as that of the young martyrs, and which — to quote a very different kind of example — was what drove Thérèse of Lisieux to disregard all human injunctions and speak directly to the Pope when she wanted permission to enter the Carmel at fifteen. Surrounded by the Thuringian court, no wonder Elizabeth was solitary.

The little Hungarian princess on that Feast of the Assumption clearly revealed herself as a person chosen by God for His own purpose, and such a call has to be followed. A vocation is nearly always terrible and wonderful, but it is still more terrible to refuse it.

Such a challenge must always awake opposition as indeed our Lord said it would, not only from what is bad in "the world," but even from the good. Prudence comes into play, and just as Bishop Guido and the Pope had to be prudent with Saint Francis, so the Landgräfin Sophie had a certain justification of prudence when she took the child to task for this public exhibition. She was not an irreligious woman; indeed she probably had it already in her mind to retire to the Cistercian monastery in Eisenach. Fundamentally her piety agreed with Elizabeth, but she could not tolerate such an expression of devotion even to our Lord. Perhaps the Landgräfin subconsciously felt the challenge and the reproof it entailed, and this brought an added note of sharpness into her voice. Does not the child Elizabeth challenge all our failings due to human respect?

It is a fact that the earliest known sources do not insist on her persecution by her mother-in-law; that came somewhat later. They all admit, however, that she had a very hard time, and persecution can take many forms; there are so many ways of hurting a child and making life a burden. Guda says distinctly that Elizabeth was disliked on account of her piety, especially it seems by Agnes who may have been jealous of her. Any person whose very being as well as behavior is a standing challenge and reproof to everyone else is rarely popular, until the force and beauty of sanctity asserts itself with an invincible attraction. At that particular moment little Mechthilde of Magdeburg, five years younger than Elizabeth, was having an unhappy, friendless childhood, and though these two did not know each other they were kindred spirits.

A certain clash of personalities was inevitable in the Wartburg, even if one was a mature woman and the other a child. The Landgräfin Sophie was the mistress, a great feudal lady with a deep sense of duty and responsibility, virtuous, probably beloved, surely rather like a medieval Queen Mary. Her conventional, conservative outlook demanded from all around her that form and manners should be observed, in piety as in everything else, for these she considered pillars of the social structure. It was not her fault that she could not keep pace with Elizabeth's vocation; in this she was left behind exactly as was Pietro Bernardone whose very love for his son Francis on the human plane prevented him from understanding that son's spiritual call. Sanctity is pitched both higher and deeper than goodness.

Elizabeth equally suffered acutely from having to conform to the rigid social code insisted on by the Landgräfin, who probably argued that the child was quite old enough to realize her place and obligations. It was intolerable that she should want to play with poor children and bring them into the castle on an equal footing with herself, intolerable that she should be perpetually running into the kitchen for food to give away, and perhaps Agnes and the servants, probably on their mistress' side, were not above telling tales. Anyhow Elizabeth must learn to behave like a young princess and the Landgräfin Sophie minced neither words nor punishments when she was disobeyed. As to the child's excessive piety, no one in the Wartburg needed her to teach them their duty to God.

With Hermann's death the whole question of Ludwig's marriage again came up, and from their point of view it can hardly be wondered at if some of the relations and nobles and retainers were against the engagement with Elizabeth. Agnes can be trusted to have been very sharp at picking up, and repeating unkind gossip. The fact was that Elizabeth's circumstances had changed. She had come to Thuringia as a rich princess, but Gertrude of Hungary was dead and who was to carry out her promise to add to her daughter's dowry? King Andreas had promptly remarried as his second wife, Yolande, daughter of Pierre de Courtenay, count of Auxerre, and the sister of two Latin Emperors of Constantinople. On the death of one of his brothers-in-law Andreas was put forward as a possible Emperor, but the Pope instead of consenting reminded him that his vow of the Crusade was still unfulfilled. So Pierre de Courtenay got himself crowned, but he died, and the succession passed to his son Robert.

At last Andreas seemed to be seriously considering the Crusade, which was to be paid for by new taxes and loans; he gave up Zara and entrusted the education of Elizabeth's brother Bela to their uncle Berthold, who had become bishop of Aquileia. John, archbishop of Gran, was left as regent of Hungary, the Grand Master of the Templars, regent of Croatia and Dalmatia, and Andreas set sail accompanied by Duke Leopold of Austria and two other of Elizabeth's uncles, Otho, duke of Meran, and Eckbert, bishop of Bamberg.

They landed at Acre and were received with lavish entertainment. The truce between Christians and Mohammedans had ended in 1217, and the campaign began. It was a complete failure, the troops were decimated by hunger and plague and Andreas fell ill. Meanwhile anarchy reigned in Hungary and Serbia had fallen away from the crown. Among Andreas' more foolish acts was to promise the Grand Master of the Knights of Saint John rights on the Hungarian salt mines and these surpassed Elizabeth's whole dowry.

In Hungary things went from bad to worse; Andreas' other son, Coloman, Prince of Galicia, at the age of nine was ousted from his dominions and finally taken prisoner by the Russians. In his feverish search for money to pay his mercenaries the King refused to pay his sister-in-law Constance the sum due to her, and he also seized the money she had left in charge of the Knights of Saint John; as another bad expedient he sold some of the crown lands to his barons. The Pope supported Constance over her claim, but that tangle was cut through by her death.

All this naturally was known in the Wartburg, and it was at least partly true that Elizabeth was no longer a brilliant worldly and financial match for Ludwig. His vassals argued that he could do much better for himself by repudiating her and marrying into one of the other great families of the German princes. Elizabeth must have realized a good deal of all this, and no one seems to have had many qualms as to the happiness or misery of a defenseless child. The lesson princesses had to learn was that they were pawns in the political game. In this case, however, there was something else. Ludwig and Elizabeth had always called each other Brother and Sister, and evidently Elizabeth felt with the full violence of her nature that they were made to be together. Thierry of Apolda says that "God had marvelously inclined Ludwig's heart toward her."

Later writers laid great stress on Elizabeth's longing for virginity and suggest that she was married against her will, but that is certainly not the impression given by the account of her intimate friends when telling about this phase of her life. No shadow of doubt seems to have crossed her mind that in loving Ludwig she was obeying the will of God, and therefore loving Him. When she knew that there was a danger of her being parted from Ludwig she threw herself into blind, violent trust in God; what self-control and what determination she showed. The Landgräfin might tell her she was only fit to be a servant, or when irritated by Elizabeth's long prayers and passionate generosity that she had better go and be a nun; nothing mattered except whether or not Ludwig cared for her.

He had one little sign which meant the world to her. Whenever he went away he always brought her back a present. She would run to meet him and triumphantly hug the gift. Then came a day when the trumpets announced his arrival; Elizabeth bounded down the steps laughing and confident. He had brought two guests with him and was swinging himself off his horse: "Why, I've forgotten your present." How vivid the scene is; it might be happening today, and not be just a trifle which happens to have been recorded seven hundred years ago.

Among Elizabeth's faithful servants was Sir Walther of Vargila who had received her into his arms from her father, and he may have comforted her in the episode of the present; she may even have asked his help.

One day he was riding alone with Ludwig and begged if he might ask a question and receive an answer.

"Go on," said Ludwig, "if I can, I will answer."

"My Lord, do you wish to keep the daughter of the King of Hungary and marry her, or do you wish to send her back to her own country?" They were facing the Inselberg, the highest hill of Thuringia. Ludwig pointed to it: "Do you see that hill? If it were entirely of good red gold and belonged to me, I would rather give that up sooner than Elizabeth. Let people talk; I love her, and she is dearer to me than anything."

"May I tell her this, my Lord?"

"Yes, and you can give her this as a token."

He took a small mirror from his pocket; on one side it was plainly polished, on the other engraved with the passion of Christ.

When Elizabeth received the mirror she was overjoyed and "warmly thanked the good Sir Walther."

Ludwig's attitude must have gone a long way to right the balance, and realizing that his mind was made up the Landgräfin would naturally have been all the more anxious to inculcate into Elizabeth the niceties of courtly manners and deportment, how to dress, how to make up, how to eat, sit, walk, look, bow and curtsy, how to answer a knight who wished to take you for his lady, how to give him your glove or your sleeve, how to give orders to the servants, and manage the house, how to behave in church just as much as in the Rittersaal. To the Landgräfin these were rightly important matters.

By Thuringian law a prince came of age at twelve, and in the very year of his Father's death Ludwig was officially recognized as "Dei gratia Thuringiae Lantgravias et Saxonie Comes Palatinus." Presumably he did homage to Frederick as his vassal and was immediately involved in the last campaign against Otho who was again defeated and died in 1218, aged 36.

On his accession to power Ludwig had every right to be knighted, and the usual procedure of waiting for a Jungkherr to be 21 before the ceremony was an elastic rule. Ludwig was prepared in every way and had already shown how deeply he understood the knightly precepts: "My soul belongs to God, my life to my sovereign Lord, my heart to my Lady, my honor to me." Ludwig's whole relation to Elizabeth has to be seen in the light of chivalry with woman as an inspiring light. In the case of princes it was customary for other young nobles to be knighted with their ruler; together they watched their arms all night in the church, and this vigil was of great importance. When the day came they were dressed in a white tunic and girdle signifying purity, with a red cloak as the symbol of the blood they must be ready to shed in a just cause. After the Gospel at high Mass, the officiating bishop — in this case the Bishop of Naumberg — pointed out in his sermon the duties of new knights. He must hear Mass each day, and risk his life in defense of the Church and the Faith, must defend the widow and orphan, take arms to free the innocent whomsoever he might be, but he must also avoid all unjust wars. He must obey his sovereign Lord and lead an exemplary life free from sin in the eyes of God and man. "If thou dost humbly obey the laws of chivalry, know that thou wilt acquire honor in this world, and in the next eternal life."

The bishop then took the young man's hands, shutting them into the Missal at the Gospel of the day while he took the oath: "I swear to observe the rule of the holy Gospel which my hand is touching." Then the bishop hit him lightly on the shoulder: "To the honor of God I consecrate thee a Knight." He was then girded with the sword and the golden spurs.

The Church was packed with knights and ladies, the Landgräfin Sophie, the princes and princesses, and the whole court were in their places, the Mass was sung in the full beauty of medieval music, and the sun came glancing through the stained glass windows on to Ludwig as he stood there, beautiful as any saint in his white and scarlet beneath the banner of Thuringia with the red and white lion emblazoned on a blue ground. Would not any girl have been carried away? — and he was Elizabeth's knight, it was her day as well as his, and when the

procession finally left the Church to return to the Wartburg the
trumpeters were sounding a fanfare, flags were waving, and
everyone was making holiday in honor of their young Lord. The
banquet might be endless but for once Elizabeth enjoyed herself and her lovely clothes, and the whole pomp and ceremony
in which Ludwig was the hero. God had set them together;
what more could the world offer?

From the contemporary accounts Ludwig was indeed a young
knight worthy of the Round Table, one that any girl might
fall in love with. They called each other Brother and Sister, but
always Elizabeth had taken Ludwig for granted as her knight,
and here he was more splendid than even she had ever dreamed.
Thierry of Apolda describes him as tall, well proportioned, good
looking, attracting all who came near him. He was kind in
speech, brave, and daring. A story is told that a lion escaped
from its cage, and Ludwig, awakened by the commotion, did
not wait to put on any armor, but dashed down to the courtyard and threatened the lion with his fist, whereupon the
animal crouched at his feet and was led back to its den. The
story sounds less improbable when we remember that Frederick
II moved about with a circus of such beasts, and perhaps his
vassals thought it correct to copy him.

Ludwig's ideal was the service of God and he would never
tolerate any blasphemy in his hearing; he was tenderhearted
and generous to those in need, he was afraid of misusing his
power and, his biographer says, very severe with himself. He
had an enviable reputation for truth and reliability, and set a
high standard of chivalry to his court.

Several anecdotes confirm this: on one occasion he was
watching the people dancing from a window in the castle and
someone pointed out a young woman, suggesting that she should
be brought to him. He refused in a fury. Again when he was
staying at another court after a banquet he found a beautiful
young woman in his room. He made Walther of Vargila turn
her out with a silver mark saying: "Even if I did not hate the

sin of adultery, I would never insult my sister Elizabeth by such disloyalty." Even allowing for the fact that these episodes are recorded by those who wished to promote Ludwig's beatification, they may quite well be true. Elizabeth had her Sir Galahad.

While there was no doubt as to Ludwig's attachment to the Faith and the Church, still he would not have been Hermann's son had he not been extremely ready to vindicate his own rights against any encroachments of the clergy's temporal power. He could have appealed to the independence of spirit of the great Saint Hildegarde who had been willing to risk excommunication in defense of what she considered justice and her own spiritual rights. Jurisdiction was always a smoldering question ready to flare up at any moment; in Ludwig's case his adversary, Siegfried of Mainz, had an excellent record as archbishop, he had founded churches and convents, whenever possible he had reconciled enemies, but he was overhasty in threatening spiritual penalties if he thought the Church's case could be advanced. Even Innocent III advised him to show greater patience and caution. When Ludwig unhesitatingly rejected the Archbishop's claim to suzerainty over certain fiefs in Hesse and Thuringia he was declared excommunicated, and this was the occasion when Siegfried stated that Hermann had died in the same state.

Excommunication. The word must have dropped like a stone into Elizabeth's heart. It was nothing new to the Wartburg — indeed it was a weapon frequently used to coerce princes in their many struggles with the higher clergy, generally over questions of feudal jurisdiction. Now it had fallen on Ludwig, Elizabeth's own knight, and it meant privation of the outward means of grace, darkness, and division from the Church he had sworn to defend. Ludwig, too, must have suffered, but not as much as Elizabeth. The secular prince in him answered the sentence by pushing on his preparations to invade the archbishop's territory, and because he was efficient and energetic he took Siegfried by surprise and devastated the lands of Merenburg and Scharfenstein. The Archbishop sued for peace through the abbots of Fulda and Hersfeld, and the reconciliation took place in the church of Saint Boniface in 1219 when the excommunication was lifted.

In the following year the Archbishop and Ludwig met again when Frederick called a meeting of the German Princes in Frankfurt to elect his son Henry King of the Germans while he proceeded to receive the imperial crown in Rome. Siegfried's and Ludwig's hackles seem to have risen at the sight of each other, but Frederick insisted that his plans would be jeopardized if they did not keep the peace, and he was not a sovereign to tolerate a subject's refusal. Some arrangement was made, connected perhaps with a large sum of money which the Archbishop paid to the Landgraf not long afterward.

From the moment of his accession Ludwig was more or less embroiled in warfare and in the restless politics of the time. This perhaps accounts for the fact that there is no mention in any chronicle of the exact date of his marriage. At the latest it must have been in the early summer of 1221 when he was 21 and Elizabeth fourteen.

In that same year the Landgräfin Sophie wrote to Pope Honorius III to inform him that she wished to remain a widow, and would live with the Cistercian nuns of Saint Catherine in Eisenach, following a mitigated form of their rule. She wished, however, to retain control of her own property in order to compensate those who had been unjustly deprived of their goods by her husband. This certainly suggests that Ludwig and Elizabeth were already married.

CHAPTER IV

THE BRIDE

THE wedding festivities and three days' tournament were over when all Eisenach had been again *en fête*, and flags and flowers and acclamations had greeted the young couple. Dressed in the richest damask with a magnificent velvet mantle, a crown on her head, and wearing the Hungarian jewels, Elizabeth knew the joy of being a beautiful bride, a lady every knight would wish to serve. As Landgräfin she stepped into an assured place among the great ladies of Europe, and her and her husband's life was linked to the cosmopolitan network of feudal politics and society. The Wartburg and Landgräfenhof hummed with activity; constant guests had to be entertained with all the refinements of courtly custom, with feasting, jousting, hunting, songs, dancing, and music; there was also the whole business of government and politics to be carried on, and Ludwig was a very busy, very competent, and rather aggressive young man.

Elizabeth's friend Isentrude tells us that "she lived with her husband in a bond worthy of all praise." Her spontaneity, her directness were those of a child; she loved Ludwig, and when that word is used in connection with Elizabeth, it means total self-donation. Above all else she enjoyed being with him, sitting at his side in the great hall, riding with him, a falcon on her wrist, and she threw herself into his life. If he liked seeing her in beautiful clothes, she wore them, though he did not know of the hair shirt she also habitually had next to her skin. When Ludwig had to be away, as often happened, and it was impossible for her to go too, she dressed as a widow until his return, the very picture of the disconsolate lady into whose mouth the Minnesingers put so many of their songs. At the first sound of the trumpet announcing his arrival she rushed to meet him, "covering his mouth with a thousand kisses." This deep human devotion as it emerges from the earliest records seems to me an integral element in Elizabeth's being, expressed in her own words: "It is in God that I love my husband; may He who sanctified marriage grant us eternal life."

There was, however, another and equally obvious side to her life, for her marriage enabled her to give still freer rein to the lavish generosity, sympathy, and kindness which were fundamental to her nature. She gave with both hands, and had she possessed eight, they would still have been insufficient. As lady of the castle she could do more for the poor who flocked to the gate even without overstepping the conventions, and when these got in her way she just paid no attention to them. It is only too likely that conservative vassals and servants shook their heads, well knowing what to expect with Elizabeth as mistress. Even if the Landgräfin Sophie was living in the monastery in Eisenach, she was quite near enough to hear what was going on, and as far as respect for etiquette went her bringing up of her daughter-in-law had been very unsuccessful. Agnes too may have been hostile to Elizabeth.

Most of the poor and sick who came to the castle were helped by Elizabeth in person. What did she care when someone remonstrated with her for dressing a beggar's horrible sores in an out of the way corner of the building, or when she was found tenderly nursing a terribly infected head from which she had just cut away the hair. Did the objectors really expect her to regard their ideas as more important than someone else's pain? What appeared so incomprehensible to her attendants was her obvious happiness in doing all this. "She was laughing . . . she was gay . . . she accomplished all her works of charity with great joy of soul, and her face never changed." Elizabeth must have been irresistible, but I expect many of us would have sided with the Landgräfin Sophie and the servants. Each day carried Elizabeth's challenge a step further.

A rather later charming legend tells how one day on her way down to Eisenach she was besieged by a crowd of beggars and had soon given away all that she had with her, so that she had nothing left for another beggar who piteously besought her charity. She could not bear to disappoint him, so gave him one of her gloves embroidered with jewels. A young knight saw it, and promptly bought the glove which he placed on his helmet as a sign of divine protection. He became a famous Crusader, and as an old man told how he attributed his safety in many battles to Elizabeth's glove.

Active as she was, when she heard of bad cases among the people of Eisenach she went to see for herself what they lacked; evil smells, distressing sights were nothing in comparison with her desire to help. She knew what the poorest houses were like, how her people lived, what it meant to be ground down by poverty. She paid debts, she brought food, money, clothes, she helped to clean, to nurse, to lay out the dead, and it all seemed inadequate beside the unending need. She had to do it, her radiant youth had to be turned on the many dark corners, for above all Elizabeth cared desperately about other people. It was her vocation, and as such a challenge to the whole feudal world. Everyone understood the call of a nun, even of such a visionary and reformer as Saint Hildegarde or such a contemplative as Saint Elizabeth of Schoenau, but this was something quite different. What was Elizabeth trying to do? Many feudal lords and ladies were very generous; none but Elizabeth gave herself in the most natural, direct, and spontaneous way possible.

The challenge could not have been more pointed and subtle since it was delivered to her own world by one of themselves. On one side was the rich, powerful feudal society, on the other Elizabeth. Most of her contemporaries were so busy with politics, society, and their own lives that they did not stop to think of how other people lived. The feudal lords were steadily becoming richer, but who remembered that the luxury of the courts was paid for by extortionate oppression of the poor? In the exciting inrush of luxury stuffs from the East new fashions appeared, and here was Elizabeth exhorting the ladies of Eisenach to moderate their extravagance, curtail the richly embroidered oversleeves that were all the fashion, even imploring them not to dance. Naturally many eyes were turned on the Wartburg and many tongues wagged. The extraordinary thing was that according to the earliest records Ludwig did nothing to hamper, and even encouraged, her.

Isentrude, who lived with Elizabeth for about five of her six years of marriage, described that life to the examiners in the Cause of Canonization. She insisted on Elizabeth's unfailing and devout piety and her attachment to prayer. We still see the impetuous little girl in Isentrude's statement that the ladies in waiting complained because Elizabeth was always in a hurry to get to church, and invariably arrived there before anyone else. Ludwig, too, heard Mass every day, and Isentrude makes us feel very close to them when she tells of his anxiety that Elizabeth would be overtired with such long prayers, and that he often held her hand while she was praying. She liked to get up in the night to pray, and Ludwig, even if not asleep, would pretend to be so as not to disturb her. Not always able to wake herself, Elizabeth made Isentrude promise to pull her foot. This plan seemed to work, but one night Ludwig crossed his leg over his wife's, and consequently was the one to have his foot pulled. However, when he was told the reason with many apologies he took it good-naturedly. We almost hear the young voices laughing. Sometimes during her long prayers Elizabeth fell asleep on the floor. When asked why she had not got back into bed she answered: "Since I cannot pray unceasingly, I can at least mortify my flesh by separating myself from the husband I love."

Elizabeth's first child was born on March 28, 1222, during one of Ludwig's absences and was baptized Hermann after his grandfather. In that same year the Reinhardsbrunn chronicle tells us that Ludwig and Elizabeth went to Hungary accompanied by Heinrich von Schwarzburg, Heinrich von Stahlberg, Ludolf von Berlstadt, Reinhard Varch, and Rudolf the Cupbearer, and no doubt a company of attendants and men-at-arms. Their way lay by Prague, but again it seems unlikely that Elizabeth met her cousin Agnes. The latter's first fiancé, Prince Boleslas of Poland, had died as a boy, and she had been brought back to a monastery of Premonstratensian nuns in Bohemia. It seems uncertain whether Elizabeth's aunt Constance was still alive but King Otokar, an important figure in central European politics, could congratulate himself that the marriage he had encouraged between Ludwig and Elizabeth was now an accomplished fact. He counted on Thuringian support for Bohemia.

The reason for the journey to Hungary is not stated; perhaps Ludwig wanted to see for himself the state of Hungary and his father-in-law's finances. He and Elizabeth were magnificently received at the Hungarian court and one cannot help wondering how much Elizabeth remembered, what likeness did her father trace in his daughter, and what was her meeting with him. As usual Andreas was in trouble, and had lately been obliged to grant his nobles considerable privileges which curtailed the royal power. As usual, too, there were family difficulties. Bela, then sixteen and Elizabeth's eldest brother, already had a party in favor of putting him on the throne; the rift was widened by Queen Yolande's dislike of Bela's wife, a Greek princess. In Elizabeth's life where time is so precious it interests us to know how she spent even a few months, but the Hungarian visit passes like a shadow; both her father and her brother outlived her.

Whenever it was possible Elizabeth accompanied Ludwig to his different castles when he moved about administering justice, and the young Landgräfin was everywhere feted, meeting people of her own rank, hearing the news and talk of the day. It is relevant to remember what Saint Francis of Sales said of her: "Saint Elizabeth of Hungary played and danced, and frequented assemblies of recreation, without any detriment to her devotion, for this was so deeply rooted in her soul that it increased amid the pomps and vanities to which her state exposed her, as the rocks in the lake of Riette are said to grow larger amidst the waves which beat against them. Great fires are increased by the wind, while small ones are extinguished, if not screened from it."

There were constant political troubles to be smoothed out or fought over. In 1221 Dietrich, Markgraf of Misnia and the husband of Ludwig's half-sister Jutta, died, leaving Ludwig as guardian to his son Heinrich, which shows Dietrich's respect for his brother-in-law. Ludwig summoned Dietrich's vassals to do homage to Heinrich and to himself, and he demanded that if Heinrich should die prematurely the succession was to be his. Only Bishop Ekkehard of Merseburg demurred, and when Ludwig insisted the Bishop excommunicated him, placing the country under an interdict. The ban was lifted only after lengthy negotiations; Ludwig paid the Bishop an indemnity, but he won on all the major points of the tussle, and was recognized as Regent for his nephew.

The Church had no more loyal son than Ludwig in the spiritual sphere, but in the matter of territorial and political questions he faced any bishop as another secular ruler and nothing else. Sometimes he pushed this attitude to extremes as when the Bishop of Meissen appealed to the Emperor, accusing Ludwig of having laid hands on his salt mines. In that discussion Frederick supported the Bishop, and on another occasion we find Ludwig taking the Bishop's side in a controversy about tithes. All these happenings are woven into the background of Elizabeth's life.

Jutta and her nobles seem to have found Ludwig too domineering, and she secretly arranged to marry Poppon von Henneberg. Ludwig was furious at not having been told of the engagement, and in the ensuing skirmishes he razed the fortress of Leipzig to the ground. Jutta complained bitterly of her brother with whom she was soon at war, and again Ludwig conquered, having naturally inflicted appalling hardships on the people whose land served as a battlefield. He demanded his nephew as hostage, and peace was only definitely re-established through the good offices of Duke Otho of Meran, Elizabeth's uncle. During the campaign Ludwig spent Easter in Dresden; one wonders whether Elizabeth was with him.

That same year saw another political commotion when the King of Denmark and his son were made prisoners by Heinrich von Schwerin. It was a complicated question involving fiefs which Frederick II had given to King Waldemar, who in his turn had ceded them to Albrecht von Orlamünde, the husband of Ludwig's other half-sister Hedwig. With the King a prisoner, the moment seemed propitious for Frederick to take back the fiefs to the detriment of Ludwig's brother-in-law. Supported by his uncle the Duke of Bavaria the Landgraf played an important part in the long drawn out negotiations, and this brought him into still closer touch with the Emperor. The two young men seem to have understood each other, and this is interesting because it draws Elizabeth and Frederick closer; plans for a Crusade were being discussed, and it seemed likely that Ludwig would join it.

Another matter of family interest was the question of the marriage of Agnes of Bohemia. It was now suggested that she should marry Frederick's son Heinrich, and she was sent to an Austrian convent to learn the niceties of German court manners. At the same time the eldest son of Duke Leopold of Austria was affianced to that other Agnes, Elizabeth's playmate and Ludwig's sister. Leopold, however, set another plan on foot which was to marry his daughter Margaret to Heinrich of Hohenstaufen in the place of Agnes. This idea of an Austrian marriage for his heir appealed to Frederick more than that with Agnes of Bohemia, and evidently Ludwig was again useful as a diplomat since the Duke of Austria consented to accept Agnes of Thuringia as his son's bride without a dowry. Naturally Otokar of Bohemia was annoyed when his daughter was sent back from Austria, although Agnes had every chance of making a brilliant marriage, for Henry III of England asked for her hand, and so did Frederick II for himself after the death of his second wife. Agnes, however, had other ideas; she was sick of royal matchmaking, and wrote to Pope Gregory IX asking to be taken under his protection because she wished to make a vow of virginity. She could not know what the next few years were to hold both for herself and for her cousin.

Elizabeth's second child, a daughter, had been born in the Wartburg on March 24, 1224, and baptized Sophie after her grandmother; then in the following year the Austrian and Thuringian royal families met in Nuremberg for the gorgeous weddings of King Heinrich and Margaret of Austria, and Heinrich of Austria and Ludwig's sister Agnes of Thuringia. The young Thuringian Landgraf and Landgräfin must have been a beautiful couple among all the other princes, and an attractive story is told of how Ludwig gave a great banquet in honor of the marriage. The guests were already assembling and still Elizabeth did not appear; Ludwig went to fetch her and found her beautifully dressed indeed but without her long court mantle. With her ladies standing around she confessed that she had given it to a beggar; would Ludwig be angry? She did not need to be told that no lady could be seen in society without such a cloak. At that very moment one of her ladies came to say that after all the mantle was hanging in its accustomed place.

The festivities ended on a tragic note: news came that King

Heinrich's guardian, the Archbishop Engebert, had been assassinated, and in a court of justice summoned by the young king to indict the murderers a staircase gave way killing a number of people.

Shortly afterward Ludwig was again at war, this time with Duke Heinrich of Silesia, the husband of Elizabeth's saintly Aunt Hedwig, on account of territories which he considered as belonging to his ward, the young Markgraf of Misnia, and again he was successful. There was no doubt that it was advantageous to have the Landgraf Ludwig as a friend.

Alongside of these family and political excitements something else extremely important had been happening. The first Franciscans had appeared in Germany.

Already in 1217, at a Chapter held at the Porziuncula, that is Saint Mary of the Angels near Assisi, it had been determined to send missionaries to countries beyond Italy. According to Francis' wish they were to carry no credentials, no authorization, and to go armed only with the Cross and the Gospel. He sent them out with the words: "In the name of the Lord go forth two and two in all humility and modesty . . . pray to the Lord and let no idle word be spoken amongst you. Though you be walking abroad let your conduct be as humble and becoming as in a hermitage or cell. Wherever we are or wherever we travel we have our cell with us. Brother Body is our cell and the soul is the hermit who dwells within to pray and meditate upon the Lord. Of little use is a cell made with hands if the soul is not at rest in its own cell."

The mission to Germany was led by John of Penna; not one of the friars knew a foreign language or had any idea of the habits of other countries. They picked up the word "Ja," which answered well when some kindly people asked whether they wanted food. Unfortunately the next question was whether or not they were heretics from Lombardy, and when again they replied "Ja," they were driven away with a beating. The mission was a complete failure, and in Hungary things went even worse: "the brethren were compelled to flee from divers provinces, and thus straitened and afflicted, sometimes robbed and beaten by thieves, they returned in great bitterness of spirit to Blessed Francis" (3 Soci. 62).

Four years later the question came up at another General Chapter, but meanwhile the Holy See had decreed that missionaries must carry credentials, to which Francis unwillingly consented. Francis was too ill to speak at the Chapter, but he sat at Brother Elias' feet and told him what to say: "My brothers, there is a country called Germany where pious Christians live who often come to our country to visit the tombs of the saints, sweating under the sun with long staves and candles and singing the praise of God. Since the brothers who last went to them suffered ill-treatment the Brother (as Francis was habitually called) does not force anyone to return there. To those, however, who wish to go, filled with love of God and zeal for souls, the Brother promises the same merit of obedience as to those who go overseas. Any brothers wishing to go to Germany, come and stand on this side." Brother Giordano da Giano, who describes the scene, continues: "ninety rose up all filled with the desire of martyrdom. There was a certain brother present who prayed that his faith should not fail through the heresies of the Lombards and the cruelties of the Germans. He did not want to go, but regretting that he had not personally known five other brothers who had lately been martyred in Morocco, he went round the group speaking to each in order to be able to boast of having known a martyr." Poor Giordano — for it was of himself that he wrote — did not get off so easily. One of the ninety, Brother Palmerius of Apulia, caught hold of Giordano saying: "You must come with us." Giordano struggled to free himself, but when Brother Caesar of Spires, a German himself, started to choose whom he would take, he pointed to brother Giordano, who promptly refused. Brother Caesar insisted, and when the matter was referred to Brother Elias, then Minister General, he ratified Brother Caesar's choice. Brother

Giordano of Giano in his delightful chronicle told the story himself many years later when he was Provincial of Thuringia.

There set out for Germany twelve priests and fifteen lay brothers, among them Thomas of Celano, the biographer of both Saint Francis and Saint Clare, and the composer of the *Dies Irae,* that great missionary Giovanni di Pian Carpine, Abraham of Hungary, Conrad, and Barnabas. They traveled by way of Botzen, Brixen, Sterzing, and the Brenner, a formidable route for winter. Their first headquarters was in Augsburg, but they divided into groups, Giordano and two others went to Salzburg, three others to Ratisbon, Giovanni di Pian Carpine led another detachment northwest to Würzburg, Mainz, Worms, Speyer, Strassburg, and Cologne.

In Germany as in Italy and southern France the friars found a widespread desire for the life of the Gospel which many people thought could be attained by following one or other of the innumerable heretical sects. Many of these were Manichaean in origin, others came into being through local discontent at abuses among the clergy which encouraged enthusiasm for a spiritual life independent of priests. Cologne, for instance, was a hotbed of heresy, so much so that the orthodox attributed the terrible earthquake of 1222 to this backsliding.

In the new preachers people found men just as enthusiastic for the gospel life as any heretic, but who not only supported the clergy, but would not even preach without their permission. This in itself was enough to attract attention, and on the whole they were well received. People were touched by their simplicity, and the Italians among them soon learned to say *"Brod durch God"* when they were famished. Giordano, in writing his chronicle, still remembered the comic episodes of the first adventurous days in Germany and recalls the kindness shown to the Brothers. He accounts for the failure of the earlier mission by saying that the time for success had not yet come.

Caesar of Spires was an excellent preacher, and quite soon at Würzburg he received a new brother into the Fraternity,

Hartmut, whom the Italians, finding his name difficult, called Andreas since he had joined them on that Apostle's feast. With him came a lay brother Rüdiger, and within a few years Andreas became guardian of a convent in Saxony while Rüdiger went with Giovanni di Pian Carpine to see Bishop Conrad of Hildesheim, who gave permission for the friars to preach and hear confessions in his diocese. A chapter of the Brothers was held in Speyer, near to a leper settlement, and it was decided to send Brothers to Saxony and Franconia; not very long after this Albert of Pisa was so struck by the friar's success in Saxony that on his way through Thuringia he established a group in Erfurt, and again we hear that they lodged near the lepers. Late in 1223 all the Brothers had the satisfaction of knowing that their Rule had at last been formally approved by Pope Honorius III.

Thus the life begun in Assisi was gradually drawing near to the Wartburg. It is quite likely that Elizabeth had already heard of Francis through Frederick II, who is said to have had an interview with him when Francis returned from the East in 1221. If this is so, then that meeting must indeed have been remarkable with the Poverello and Stupor Mundi facing each other. A meeting with Francis never seems to have meant collision, and certain incidents in Frederick's later life seem to show his influence. It would certainly have interested Frederick to hear of Francis' interview with the Sultan.

There was something in Francis, and in the First Companions' expression of his ideal, which appealed to the rich and powerful just as much as to the poor. Francis delivered his message into the rough and tumble of contemporary life and politics as well as to the downtrodden, and from the beginning he made converts and recruits among the learned and the rich. Among the first companions there were Brothers from all walks of life; many others followed. Francis offered the Gospel to everybody, and the response was colossal. These people were not asked to follow a rule but to live the Gospel as he had proposed in his Letter to All Christians. It was a great reaching out to those masses he would never see, but about whom he cared so much. The whole letter breathes the Gospel, and much of it consists in quotations; it is a burning appeal to share in the joy of following Christ, to turn from the misery of sin. "To us it is open to be the mother, the brother, the sister, the spouse of Christ when by the Holy Spirit the faithful soul is united to him. O how glorious, and holy and great it is to have a Father in Heaven! O how holy, how beautiful and lovable to have a Spouse in Heaven! O how holy, how beloved, how pleasing and humble, peaceful and sweet to have such a Brother Who laid down His life for His sheep, and prayed for us to the Father: Holy Father keep them in Thy Name whom Thou hast given Me." After a passionate exhortation to praise God and avoid vice, avarice being specially mentioned, Francis begs that all will receive this letter, and that those who cannot read will have it read to them, and he ends: "And all both men and women who shall receive these things kindly, and understand and send them to others for an example, if they persevere in them unto the end, may the Father, Son and Holy Ghost bless them. Amen."

In this letter we almost hear Francis' voice, preaching, talking, convincing. This was the message his followers were to deliver, and if the friars brought any document with them to Germany it would have been this letter which Francis so explicitly says is directed to all Christians. It would have formed the subject matter of their preaching, and everywhere they went people heard of it; when they reached Thuringia would not Elizabeth have felt it as a direct message to her?

Brother Rüdiger seems to have been the first to enter the Wartburg; within a short time he became guardian of the friars in Halberstadt and Elizabeth's spiritual director. At that moment a new note in her sanctification seems to have been part of God's design.

Elizabeth, of course, heard far more than the letter. Here

indeed was someone to whom the friars could pour out the story of Francis, of Clare, of Rivotorto, and the Porziuncula and the wonderful awakening among people of all sorts and kinds. "He loves Our Lord as no one else; he lives the Passion and weeps continually over the sufferings of Christ; he wants even our habits to be in the shape of a Cross; he carries Jesus in his heart, and gives Him to us; his penance is never ending and he is the most joyful man alive; he loves everything for love of God, every man, woman, child, lepers, robbers, princes, infidels, for him they are all children of God; he loves every animal, every created thing, why we've seem him preaching to birds, talking to hares, lifting up worms to save them from being crushed, he wants to live, and for us to live as Christ did with His disciples; we respect everyone, above all the clergy of our Holy Mother Church; we have seen Brother Francis kneel before any priest and kiss his hands because no reverence is too great for him who consecrates the sacred Host and touches the Body of God's Son; Francis calls us his Minores and we want, like him, to be the Lesser ones with no honors and no riches; he accepts all who want to follow him; in every place he reconciles enemies and drives out the devils of discord; he sends us in his place to do the same, and to bring to all the same greeting, *Pax et Bonum,* good people, the Lord give you peace."

Again one almost hears the voices.

Peace. The word had never sounded so alive; peace in a world which in Elizabeth's experience was always at war. But everything in this message was new, alive, real. This was life such as she had longed for, toward which she had been groping alone, and here it was at last being actually lived. She had to hear every available detail of Francis and Bernard and the First Companions, of Clare and Giacoma de' Settesoli, who after all as a great Roman lady with husband and children had the same ties as her own. The friars could tell her of that numerous outer ring of followers to whom Francis had opened a new life, different from that of the various lay associations already in existence. He not only loved ordinary human nature but he trusted it, and under his kindling enthusiasm many people suddenly became capable of great things, of living at their best. When the whole village of Cannara came trooping after him it meant that for the moment every soul there rose to a heroic level. This episode is often quoted as the origin of the Franciscan Third Order though the town of Poggibonsi also claims the first place in its history. The friars who talked to Elizabeth may have known Lucchesio and Bonadonna. Saint Bonaventure suggests that the idea came to Francis at the Porziuncula and that "he went through the towns and villages proclaiming the Gospel and the kingdom of eternal life to all people, not with the words of human wisdom but speaking in the power of the Spirit. Because of the fire of the preaching of Blessed Francis, in many men and women was kindled the love of God, and they began to live in chastity, and to bind themselves to do penance according to the form and doctrine and rule given by God to blessed Francis, and which he, by preaching and example showed the world. These men and women he called the Brothers and Sisters of Penance, and rightly so for the way of penance is for all who go to heaven, and in this path of penitence all can walk, priests and laymen, married persons, virgins and widows, and many miracles have shown how great this order is before God."

When Elizabeth was listening to the friars Saint Bonaventure was still a baby but his words are important in the light they throw on the beginning of what came later to be known as the Third Order of Saint Francis. Nothing with Francis was cut and dried; he did not formulate a Rule and then invite people to live by it; he excited and inspired those he met with his own burning love which touched their hearts and kindled an answering spark. Elizabeth seemed to be meeting Francis himself in the words of those brothers; her response was as immediate and complete as Clare's, and in her the spark blazed into a fire which is still a beacon. During those days in the Wartburg when the young Landgräfin heard the story told by a ragged friar her own future was being decided, and it had an immense radius for she was chosen to be one of the chief instruments in making the Third Franciscan Order into a powerful Christian influence. Many of the miracles referred to by Saint Bonaventure were those worked by God through that young, eager hostess of Brother Rüdiger.

In Eisenach the Brothers first lodged with the Teutonic Knights, but Elizabeth was evidently active in keeping them there for Conrad of Marburg speaks of "the chapel in Eisenach where Elizabeth had placed the Friars Minor." In 1225 Brother Giordano di Giano came himself to consolidate the foundation which had been helped by the very successful preaching of Rüdiger and Hermann. Through this close contact Elizabeth must have heard what had been happening to Francis, how he had set up the Christmas Crib in Greccio, but above all of the Stigmata he had received at La Verna when our Lord set His own seal on Francis and on the vocation of his followers. What must have been the impression on Elizabeth of such a proof of the union of Francis with God?

It is inconceivable that the Brothers in Germany did not tell Francis about Elizabeth. Wadding, writing in the sixteenth century, describes their intercourse, basing his account on a manuscript in Louvain, now lost. Given the persons and circumstances the tradition seems perfectly plausible even though Thomas of Celano who was also in Germany does not mention it. From Wadding we learn that Francis often spoke of Elizabeth, and it was Cardinal Ugolino who suggested that he should send her his own cloak in token of his recognition of her help to the friars and of her own spirit of poverty. He surely saw her as filling in Germany the place of "Brother Giacoma" in Italy. It is said that Elizabeth always wore the cloak when she was praying for some special favor.

Even before the gift she had certainly put on the spirit of

Francis in the same way as did the First Companions; one might say that she was a Franciscan before she ever heard of Francis. Her approach to God had the same vibrations as his; when she found her own ideal impersonated in Francis it was to Elizabeth what the finding of the Grail was to Arthur's knights. Spiritually she was at one with him; she was being called to reflect his ideal as faithfully as Clare, and at every step her response was complete. Through her life Elizabeth had always answered God's calls one by one to the utmost of her strength at that particular moment; there was no sudden break or "conversion," but after her meeting with the friars there was a definite heightening of tension which can be traced in the outward events.

On one occasion Ludwig had invited a gay party of knights and ladies to the Wartburg, and while they were all at Mass before the Elevation Elizabeth's eyes strayed to Ludwig with a rush of human tenderness. Her attention was recalled at the Elevation by a vision of Christ Crucified with bleeding wounds in the hands of the priest. Overcome with sorrow for her distraction, and pity for the sufferings of our Lord, she threw herself at His feet in spirit with Mary Magdalene and with her face on the ground began to cry bitterly. She remained there prostrate until the dinner hour; no one dared to disturb her and at last Ludwig came himself. "Dear Sister, why won't you come and dine? Why do you keep us waiting so long?" His gentle words roused her; she got up and he saw how red and swollen her eyes were, and filled with pity he went on: "Why have you cried like this?" But he began to cry too and understood that she could not come to the feast. So, drying his own eyes, he left her to her contemplation and rejoined his guests with so glad a face that no one could have guessed what had happened (Ködiz).

On another occasion the priest saw Elizabeth's face shining transfigured after Holy Communion. This is not a very rare gift of our Lord to the saints; it is as though the body becomes transparent through the might of God's presence in the soul.

It seems to me that Elizabeth's dealings with the lepers can best be placed after her meeting with the Franciscans. Certainly the Middle Ages considered lepers with reverence remembering the text of Isaias with its prophetical description of our Lord: "A leper, so we thought him, a man God had smitten and brought low." Nevertheless the medieval regulations governing the lives of lepers were very strict, and in consideration of the widespread fear of contagion they were segregated and had to warn others of their approach with a little clapper. It was just because they were outcasts that they played so great a part in Francis' history and that of his Brothers. When, as a young man he met the leper on the road near Assisi, it would have been easy enough to throw the sufferer a coin, but how hard to kiss the outstretched hand and face! One of Francis' chief concerns was the service of lepers; whenever he got a chance he stayed with them, and one of his last miracles was the healing of the despairing leper.

When the friars arrived in Germany they seem to have lodged preferably near leper settlements, and they must have known that nothing would give such an impression of the most genuine charity as to follow Francis' example in caring for these sufferers. And we hear of Elizabeth searching out the lepers in their own settlement, supplying their needs, above all giving them the consolation of her presence. Isentrude tells how each time Elizabeth met lepers she would sit down with them, give them all she had, console and comfort them. On Holy Thursday when she performed the *Mandatum,* the Washing of the Feet, she chose lepers to represent the Apostles, she evidently encouraged them to come to the Castle for alms, and would not even Elizabeth have needed the extra spur of Francis' spirit to make her so unheeding of laws and convention? Isentrude stresses Elizabeth's joy and gaiety in performing these actions, and says "she was no more afraid of a leper than of a healthy person." Few people agreed with her. The Reinhardsbrunn chronicle tells how when she and Ludwig and the Landgräfin Sophie were in the castle of Neuenburg, after having bathed a leper and dressed his sores, Elizabeth placed him in her and Ludwig's bed. Her outraged mother-in-law fetched Ludwig: "See with what sick folk Elizabeth defiles your bed." It was a very natural reaction. She counted on his anger matching hers, but the chronicle continues: "God opened the Prince's eyes and he saw Christ Crucified lying in his bed. Moved at the sight he begged Elizabeth to bring in such sufferers more often for he had understood that it is the Lord Jesus in person who is received and cared for in His suffering members."

In all this Francis was the example, inspiration, and guide for Elizabeth just as he was for Clare. She began to see the other face of poverty, which is liberty from all earthly encumbrance, liberty to love God unhindered, and to serve Him in each needy and suffering human being. This was the lovely Lady Poverty whom Francis had taken as his bride. Our Lord and His Mother had lived in poverty; Elizabeth in her castle longed for a hovel. Soon she was busy with her ladies spinning wool for the Brothers; she spoke continually of the beauty of poverty, and Isentrude says that she would put on the oldest and poorest cloak she could find, and with a dilapidated bit of stuff on her head as a veil once said: "This is how I shall be dressed when I go out begging, and suffer adversity for God's sake."

After the birth of her little daughter she carried the baby herself to the church, and the people of Eisenach saw their Landgräfin barefooted and in a plain, woolen dress offering her child on the altar together with a lamb and candle. On her return she gave away the clothes she had worn. During the Rogation Days she appeared dressed in the same way, and instead of taking her usual seat, she went and sat among the poorest of the congregation.

Exhibitionism? A fine lady playing at poverty? Even if she did give away so much she knew she could have more money, more clothes, more food. If anyone felt tempted to make such a comment, Elizabeth herself gave the answer, and gives it also to us. It is true she was no more a beggar at that particular moment than Francis was when he begged in Saint Peter's before breaking with the world. Even to the enthusiasm of eighteen it needs great courage to throw off everything, especially in Elizabeth's position, and there may well have been a shade of apprehension in her desire for the reality of poverty. Perhaps she found reassurance in what may have seemed a pretense. It was at least an intimation to those who saw her of what was in her mind as a secret aspiration. Besides, though anyone can dress up physically and psychologically, only the grace of a divine vocation could have enabled Elizabeth to carry through the part as she did, toiling, facing everything that was unpleasant, stopping at nothing, and had there been anything more horrible to nurse than leprosy she would have run to do it. On one point only did she differ from those she helped; she had a comfortable home to go back to, and she was beginning to feel it not as a privilege but as a drawback. It was her joy, but already it had begun to be her burden.

Even Elizabeth's charity was put to the test in the terrible famine of 1226. The Reinhardsbrunn chronicle describes it as ravaging all Germany, and it had begun some three years earlier. "Because of men's sins God afflicted the people in various ways, by the danger of sudden death, and by a horrible epidemic of pestilence." Added to all this there were terrible floods such as had not been known for a very long time, and while Ludwig's lands were being devastated by these horrors he was away on affairs of state.

The winter of 1225 was exceptionally hard and long, and many of the sheep and cattle were struck down and died; there seemed no end to the disasters. Elizabeth was responsible only to Ludwig for her actions; had he been there she knew he would have been the first to empty his granaries to feed the starving people. As it was she did it for him, laying hands on the food reserves in her husband's four principalities. She was quite indifferent to hostile criticism, obstruction, and counsels of prudence from Ludwig's officials, and ruthless with the medieval black marketeer. The people were starving, the food was there, and it was in her power to give it; what more was there to be said?

She organized a daily distribution of hundreds of standard-sized loaves made in the Wartburg kitchen, supervising everything herself. If anything was left of the royal reserves, it was chiefly because the coming of summer brought a slight relief. She rode to the places within reach to do the same there, and a large building at the foot of the Wartburg hill was converted into a hospital for the sick and for others who needed special attention and extra food. Berthold tells us that there were twenty-eight beds, and any vacancy was filled at once. More than ever Elizabeth cleaned, nursed, laid out the dead; all her thought, her possessions, her own physical strength were concentrated in the effort to help her people. She not only wished to appear, but to be one of them; she felt herself to be the mother of her people.

She sold her jewels, and for once they seemed worth having. Isentrude says that when she and the other ladies of the court could hardly bear the sights and sounds and smells, Elizabeth was unperturbed and gay. In this sea of misery she could still think of buying toys for a number of derelict children she had collected to mother, and always the worst cases and the most defenseless children were her favorites. Isentrude also tells that she took the worst sufferers up to the castle in order to be able to look after them better. If anyone had to go short of anything, it was Elizabeth and her ladies, not these guests. Again it is Isentrude who says that one day everything available had been distributed except a little beer, and still there were people waiting. Elizabeth took the jug and filled all the glasses, and there was the same quantity of beer left over.

It was not enough to feed people; they had also to be clothed, and the chronicles insist that all this was done by Elizabeth with her own hand. When she had nothing else she gave them her own clothes with the practical injunction: "Don't use them for vanity, but sell them, buy what is necessary and work hard."

At last in the height of summer Ludwig returned and was given the usual ecstatic welcome by his wife: "his mother and brothers and the whole country greatly rejoiced at his safe return, but the joy of the dear Saint Elizabeth far surpassed that of the others."

She told him what had happened and what she had done; so did others and Ludwig heard plenty of complaints. The Landgräfin had been most reckless in her charity; she had demanded all the corn and barley, a great deal of money had gone as well as her jewels. "Well," said Ludwig, "let her do it. She gives for the love of God and to help the poor, and she can go on doing it so long as she leaves me the castles of the Wartburg and Neuenberg."

The moment was very badly chosen by those who wanted to incriminate her; in the first flush of an enthusiastic homecoming Elizabeth knew she had Ludwig's ear.

In this Ludwig indeed was only carrying out his usual practice, for Isentrude tells us that "he always accorded to blessed Elizabeth the liberty to accomplish whatever was for the glory of God, thus favoring the salvation of his and her soul." Elizabeth's marriage was perfect from the human point of view, and Ludwig was religious enough and generous enough to allow her to go any lengths in showing that almighty God came first. She carried her charity far and wide through her husband's domains, but we are not told whether her example galvanized many of her subjects into caring more about their neighbors.

The appalling conditions during the famine were a crucial experience for Elizabeth, bringing her face to face with many questions and doubts. She was haunted by the idea that she had enough to eat while others went hungry, she could not rest for thinking of the privations suffered by so many, of the excess of riches on one side, the grinding poverty on the other. She could see no other remedy but that of ever widening, ever increasing, understanding charity. One night when she and Ludwig were awake she told him how she had been considering what sort of life would be most profitable and enable them "usefully to serve God." She went on to explain: "If we had an acre of land and two hundred sheep, you would work the land yourself and I would milk the sheep." Ludwig smiled: "Darling Sister, if we had that acre of land and those two hundred sheep, we should be rich, not poor." It was he who repeated the conversation to Thierry, Archbishop of Treves, who in turn told it to Caesar of Heisterbach.

This story shows the intimate confidence existing between Ludwig and his wife. She knew the many burning points in government and administration which he had to consider, the difficulties caused by the fact that money was asserting itself as the commercial currency instead of goods; she knew the abuses and complaints, the misunderstandings on both sides in the whole complicated business of feudal rights, privileges, responsibilities, and legislation as well as the depths of suffering caused by endless feudal wars and disputes. Do what one might the fundamental trouble remained unchanged. How could all this be transformed into a state of things governed by the Franciscan *Pax et Bonum*? Elizabeth, with the single-minded impatience of youth, wanted a quick solution, and when one occurred to her she promptly told it to Ludwig.

Was Ludwig only trying to humor her when he turned the proposal back on to what he knew at the moment to be Elizabeth's vulnerable point? With her 200 sheep she would still be rich in comparison with someone. Besides there was a subtle compliment in the words; with the abolition of court routine, of politics, and family affairs and social gatherings that made up their life, there would no longer be anything to keep them apart. Ludwig knew perfectly well that it would be an enormous happiness to Elizabeth always to have him home for dinner after his morning's work in the field.

Elizabeth figures in two charming legends, or perhaps facts, which record the transformation of the charity of this world into the glory of heaven.

One day ambassadors arrived at the court of Thuringia from Hungary, wishing to take news of Elizabeth back to her father. Elizabeth heard of their arrival with trepidation, for she had given away every one of her rich clothes. What impression would it make if she appeared in the great hall dressed almost as a beggar? What tales would they carry back of Ludwig's treatment of her, yet what could she put on? Ludwig came to fetch her, saying that she must come down, but he too was disturbed at her appearance. Elizabeth's confidence returned: "Dear Brother, do not be anxious; you will see I shall know how to excuse myself with your guests, and taking a mantle that lay to hand and praying earnestly that God would help her she went down to the hall. Not only were the strangers delighted with the affability, the cordiality and sweetness of her manners, they were ravished by the beauty of her face, and the wonderful silk in which she was dressed, at her mantle of blue velvet sewn with pearls and the jewels she wore. They declared that they had never seen such clothes, which indeed astounded all the onlookers, and that not even the Queen of France was adorned as was the Landgräfin of Thuringia."

After the guests' departure Ludwig made haste to ask Elizabeth how she had come by the clothes. She answered: "God can do anything He wills."

The other story is the famous one of the roses, and it has all the fragrance of the Little Flowers of Saint Francis. Neither Guda, Isentrude, nor the earliest documents of Elizabeth's life mention it, but it was a commonplace of iconography not long after her death. It has sometimes been told as belonging to the early years before her marriage, but it seems natural to place the episode in the period of the famine when tradition says that some of Ludwig's officials were amazed at finding the reserves of corn unimpaired despite Elizabeth's depredations. However, in view of the criticism against her, Ludwig asked that she should temporarily desist from the luxury of giving away food. To this she agreed. Each day, of course, brought piteous cases of need, one woman was dying, another had threatened to kill herself, the children had nothing to eat. Who could resist such appeals? Certainly not Elizabeth. She gathered up what she could find, and she, Isentrude, and Guda started down the hill carrying a full hamper which they covered with Elizabeth's cloak. On the way they met Ludwig. "What have you got there?" he asked. "Dearest Brother, look for yourself," was Elizabeth's answer. He looked: "What, roses, at this time of year." It was winter. Elizabeth was taken aback: "But they aren't roses, they're loaves." Then she looked herself and saw the red and white flowers. And Ludwig recovered the hamper with Elizabeth's cloak, and bowed before her. "God willed to stand on my side; His love knows no bounds," was her comment.

A somewhat similar story is told of Saint Rose of Viterbo who lived a few years after Elizabeth, and again of her own great-niece Saint Elizabeth of Portugal, of whom the Breviary says that the money she was taking to the poor was turned into roses.

Since this lovely legend is attached to three early Franciscan saints, it seems worth while to recall the connection with roses of Saint Francis himself.

One night at Saint Mary of the Angels he was assailed by temptation which he resisted by going out and rolling in the brambles; their leaves were stained with his blood and they were turned into thornless roses. In a fresco in the chapel of the Rose Garden Saint Francis appears accompanied by two angels carrying the red and white roses to offer to our Lady on her altar in the Porziuncula.

To him all nature and every circumstance of life was sacramental, and this was the spirit he bequeathed to Clare, to Elizabeth, to all his followers. Treading in his steps they found that spirit to be true, and poverty, penance, suffering, human charity, and indeed everything became for them a sacrament of divine grace. Could any symbol be more lovely than the roses? Is it fortuitous that in the Stuttgart Psalter Hermann and Sophie are holding roses, and in Simone's fresco of Elizabeth in Assisi there are roses in her halo?

The period of 1225–1226 was a crucial one in Elizabeth's life, for it included the birth of her daughter, the worst stage of the famine, and her meeting with Conrad of Marburg. In his letter to Gregory IX after her death, Conrad says that he became her director two years before her husband's death, which brings us to the autumn of 1225, and from then onward he played a decisive part in her life which ever since has been discussed and criticized.

The first question one naturally asks is why, since Elizabeth was in close touch with the Franciscans, do we suddenly hear of a secular priest stepping into the place of Brother Rüdiger? The latter, of course, may have left Eisenach, and anyhow it was Ludwig who chose Conrad of Marburg. Did he perhaps suspect that his wife needed no spurring along Franciscan lines, and might be all the better for a little wise restraint? Besides, this Master Conrad was then at the height of his fame and had the reputation of being one of the wisest and holiest priests in Germany. Let us look at him through the eyes of his contemporaries: "At that time there were still just men of irreproachable virtue among the Bishops and Priests who by their example and sound doctrine worked to restore Christianity. Among these was the honorable and pious Master Conrad of Marburg whose exemplary life shone as a luminous star in German lands. He was a learned man, belonging to a family of the lesser nobility, and his conduct was blameless and pure; he knew the Scriptures well, was deeply attached to the Christian faith, and used his zeal to extirpate heresy and unbelief. He had complete contempt for riches, temporal goods and ecclesiastical benefices; he was content with one modest and simple ecclesiastical garment, his manners were worthy and grave, and his countenance and expression, austere. He showed himself kindly towards good Christians, but his treatment of, and justice towards unbelievers was harsh and severe." Conrad of Heisterbach adds a touch to the picture saying: "Conrad mortified his body with the harshest penances, and his ascendancy over souls was cold and hard." This is the description of a worthy, but not a lovable man, and certainly not in the Franciscan tradition.

Conrad had been among the second group of preachers commissioned by Pope Innocent III to preach the Crusade in Germany in 1215; and this choice was already a sign of Conrad's reputation, for Innocent had insisted that the preachers must be irreproachable in life as in doctrine. After Innocent's death Honorius III had taken up the Crusading plans, but with less success, for many people had become restive at the expense of these expeditions.

In 1220 at the wish of the Emperor Frederick II the direction of Crusading efforts in Germany was put into the hands of his own chaplain, Conrad, who became Bishop of Hildesheim, and again Conrad of Marburg was in the forefront of the propaganda. During all this time beside preaching the Crusade Master Conrad was also active in the repression of heresy — indeed the two went hand in hand. The Middle Ages did not consider religious tolerance as a virtue, and in many places the secular authorities in the name of Roman Law were no more tolerant of the Manichaean forms of heresy than was the Church. It was widely held that it mattered very much what a person believed, not only on account of his or her eternal salvation, but also in regard to behavior in this world. Our own contemporary history, incidentally, is teaching us the same lesson.

Infidels and heretics could be dealt with in two ways, by a Crusade and repressive legislation or by persuasion. Saint Bernard was an example of both; he believed that faith must come from persuasion and conviction, but he also believed in the Crusade, and Saint Francis was the same. A man of Conrad of Marburg's temperament had no doubt of the advantages of repression in varying degrees of severity; and even while he was staying at the Wartburg he was engaged as judge in the case of the Premonstratensian Heinrich Minnike who was later sent to the stake for his heretical doctrines. Conrad was then attached to the cathedral of Mainz; he was not a Dominican as has so often been asserted.

The loss of Damietta had been a blow to German Crusading hopes, but at last the Emperor fixed Saint John's day of 1225 for the departure of a new Crusade though the date was then postponed for another couple of years. The Pope urged the German preachers to redouble their efforts, and Conrad received orders to leave the Wartburg where he was staying and start on a preaching tour in the Bremen diocese, in order to whip up enthusiasm. Besides his zeal for the Crusade and for putting down heresy, Conrad had still sufficient energy not to leave a stone unturned in an attempt to reform the German regular and secular clergy. Evidently Ludwig was highly impressed with Conrad's piety and his single-minded efficiency, and the Pope had clearly shown his own confidence. Ludwig wanted the best he could get for Elizabeth and Master Conrad had probably unconsciously shown his best side during his stay in the Wartburg.

We can follow these various visible threads that seem to have led Conrad into the position of Elizabeth's spiritual director, yet how soon we come up against the mystery of God's purpose. Conrad of Marburg seems entirely ill adapted to her, yet he was the person who had almost complete control of her even before Ludwig's death. It is also clear that Elizabeth could have refused, for Irmentrude quotes her as saying: "I could have made a vow of obedience to one of the Bishops or Abbots who possess benefices, but it seemed to me better to do so to Master Conrad who has nothing, who is a beggar, so that in this life I may have no consolation whatever." Here we see Elizabeth taken with that side of Conrad which seemed in harmony with the poverty of Francis, but the gulf separating the two men was to be the cause of immense suffering to her; with Master Conrad the shadow of the cross fell on Elizabeth, and in that shadow she was to reach the height of glory. Her human feelings toward him seem to have been those of most other people: "If I can have such fear of a mortal man, how much more must I fear almighty God the Lord and Judge of all."

This most understandable apprehension worked in her as an argument for making the vow to Conrad, and Ludwig's only stipulation was that Conrad should have no say in what regarded his rights as Elizabeth's husband.

At about the same time she took a vow of perpetual continence should she become a widow. Given her passionate attachment to Ludwig, this was not perhaps very hard, and she had seen enough of forced diplomatic marriages to wish to avoid one. Isentrude tells us that she and Guda took the same vow with Elizabeth in the Church of Saint Catherine, the Cistercian monastery of Eisenach; evidently the ceremony was performed with some pomp and probably the Landgräfin Sophie was present with the nuns.

In his famous letter to Gregory IX after Elizabeth's death Master Conrad says that "even during the lifetime of her husband she regretted being subject to the bond of marriage," and Thierry of Apolda comments: "Although she loved her husband most deeply she regretted not having merited the honor of virginity." This is a plausible explanation of Elizabeth's state of mind, but when other writers, including Caesar of Heisterbach, tell us that Elizabeth was married against her will, other well-known facts of her life give the lie to such a statement. There is no proof that she was drawn to the cloister or to anything but to marriage with Ludwig, although she may certainly have recognized the beauty of finding all love satisfied in loving God, and even have regretted that such a call had not been hers. Isentrude describes Elizabeth's marriage in a few vivid words: "They loved each other with a marvelous love, gently exhorting and fortifying each other in praising and serving God." It was a perfect marriage and to Elizabeth nothing earthly mattered so long as she had Ludwig.

Master Conrad exerted his authority immediately and with vigor. One day, when he had summoned Elizabeth to go to a sermon, she had been detained by the arrival of her sister-in-law Guda, the Markgräfin of Misnie. There was every good reason for her to stay at home, especially as relations between Ludwig and his half-sister had been strained. Isentrude tells us that Elizabeth hastened the next day to make her excuses to Master Conrad who refused to accept them even with Elizabeth prostrate at his feet, and she and Guda, whom he probably considered as accomplices, were made to accept the discipline from him clad in penitential shirts. Already we seem to see Conrad as a victim to power, yet he, and no Saint John of the Cross, was allowed by God to become her director. She had not the spiritual consolation granted to Saint Teresa.

Conrad had not chosen to be Elizabeth's spiritual director, it is true, but once he found himself in that position he applied all his deep and narrow earnestness to the task of forming a saint. From the first he recognized that he was dealing with an exceptional person and vocation, and he saw danger in her fresh, affectionate spontaneity, in her generosity and sympathy, above all in her capacity for devotion and love, especially love. Every impulse, every hidden resource of her richly endowed nature must be directed toward God; Elizabeth had already understood this, but living in the world as she did, in constant peril of distraction, her will must be still further purified and strengthened to desire God alone. Master Conrad used a classical method of self-discipline for his penitent; he set before her the precepts of humility and patience, of detachment from all human opinion or consolation as well as from all earthly riches or pleasures or comfort. He taught her to relinquish herself to God, who must always be present in her thoughts and be the object of her love. She must thank Him continually for her own redemption through Jesus Christ and for love of Him must patiently carry any cross. Above all, she must consecrate herself entirely to God her Creator, who had destined her for His service and to enjoy Him eternally. Let her be mindful of the shortness of life and never cease from begging God's forgiveness for her sins. There was nothing new in all this; sanctity is always the result of the faithful observance of these principles made possible by divine grace. Conrad considered it his duty to see to it that Elizabeth should be preserved from anything that might distract her. In her case it hardly seemed necessary to add that in every way she must do to others as she would be done by, in other words to love her neighbor as herself. This command is always full of possibilities that vary according to time and place, and here Master Conrad took a line that was bound to cause Elizabeth extreme difficulty, for it regarded her daily food quite apart from any fasting about which he was also very severe.

He insisted that Elizabeth was to eat only of those dishes which she was quite sure came from legitimate sources; this meant that she had to know exactly whether a specific loaf was made from flour obtained from fields that were hers or Ludwig's uncontested property, and that the corn had not been extorted unfairly from the peasants. Equally she had to be sure that a particular dish of meat or game was obtained through legitimate shooting rights. In the thirteenth century such an order must have seemed absolutely preposterous; in it we can trace a political background, for Master Conrad well knew that the Landgraf had quarreled with the Archbishop of Mainz over certain territorial rights, and he was just as fierce in his support of ecclesiastical privilege against feudal aggression as he was in the suppression of heresy. Then was it right to eat the pheasant if some serf's corn or vegetables had been trampled down while knights and their followers were out hunting? Master Conrad could tacitly reprove his ecclesiastical superiors for their luxury by his own example, but his sermons against unjust feudal exactions met with a very inadequate result. It does seem as though Conrad's fanatical desire for justice blazed up when he found such an instrument in his hand as Elizabeth. Through her had come his great opportunity for imposing his will; it is not a pleasant picture, and yet to some extent Conrad was trying to protect the underdog and even working for the recognition of the human rights and needs of the serfs. The pity is that we cannot help disliking him.

Anyhow he laid down the law — Elizabeth was not to touch any even suspect dishes at her husband's table. This put her in an almost impossible position, and must have shown her how far Master Conrad was driving her in the name of duty. She who had so spontaneously deprived herself of everything for others, and who was so ready to go on doing it had to stop and consider where each morsel of food came from. Every meal must have become an ordeal; she did her best to obey, but with the best will in the world she could not always be sure whether a particular dish were legitimate, and here we meet a touching detail for sometimes it was Ludwig himself who told her. Evidently he wanted to help, not to hinder her, and also to give countenance to her behavior before his court. Perhaps, too, he wanted to reassure her and see her eat. Anyhow she had the comfort of knowing that he was not offended when she crumbled her bread and only pretended to eat, and her faithful friends did the same. They were all unwilling to wound Ludwig by this tacit criticism, but let us listen to his own words: "I would willingly do the same myself if I did not dread the malicious comments of those around me and of other people, but soon with God's help I shall make new arrangements as far as I am concerned." His love for Elizabeth brought him apparently to justify Master Conrad's order.

Elizabeth had her own dowry and in order to be able to eat a little more freely she began to use it to buy food for herself and her ladies, not always an easy matter when they were moving from one castle to another. She sometimes sent to ask

the local nobility for what she needed, not giving any reason
and letting them suppose she preferred their food to her own.
Master Conrad, however, soon stopped that. How did she know
where this food came from? Of course, she was not to eat it.
And because Elizabeth's idea of obedience was that of Francis,
she obeyed. Sometimes her dinner consisted in a few small
honey cakes; she had wished for poverty and it came to her in
this unexpected fashion. One day, sitting beside her husband,
five small birds were served which had been sent her as a
present; she ate one and sent the others to her ladies. Throughout this phase she suffered doubly through their privations;
when, for example, she knew that the food but not the drink
was legitimate she would say: "Today we can eat" or "Today
we can drink" as the case might be; when by a happy chance
both were permissible she clapped her hands delightedly:
"Hurrah, today we can both eat and drink." She and her
ladies were all under twenty.

To complete the picture of the ascetic side of Elizabeth's
life at that time we have to remember that political and family
affairs were, of course, in full swing. In the early spring of 1226
Ludwig went to Italy in response to the Emperor's summons
to a Diet in Cremona; that was during the famine. From the
days of Barbarossa the tenacious Lombards had been resolutely
against the Empire putting all possible spokes in the wheel,
and by closing the Brenner pass they blocked the approach to
Verona. Some of the German princes were stopped, but Ludwig,
always prompt, got through with Hermann of Salza the Grand
Master of the Teutonic Knights, an Order closely associated
with Thuringia.

There could hardly have been a more tremendous plunge
than to come from Thuringia into the semi-Oriental splendors
with which Frederick liked to be surrounded. The court was as
varied as the colors of its clothes; warriors, politicians, artists,
scientists, philosophers, dancing girls, elephants, panthers,
giraffes all had their assigned parts, and Frederick's genius

included that of a perfect stage manager. Few people could resist him if his mood were easy, or keep pace with the turns and bounds of his mind, or measure the sweep of his ambition and the relentless force of his will in getting what he wanted, and no one wished to incur his pitiless anger and revenge. Mounted on his black horse "Dragon," in resplendent garments he was the embodiment of irresistible power, a figure worthy of the great black eagle on the golden ground of the imperial banner.

At this time his quarrel with the Pope had not yet reached its most embittered stage. He welcomed Ludwig and Hermann; at the moment he was interested in the idea of a Crusade, so were they, and another prominent plan in their minds was the conquest of Prussia for which they wanted Frederick's explicit backing. Both the Pope and the Grand Master trusted the Emperor's decision for the Crusade, and indeed one of his immediate objectives was to become ruler of Jerusalem. He had made a good step toward this in the previous year by marrying Isabelle, daughter and heiress of John of Brienne, King of Jerusalem. The marriage had been possible through the death of Frederick's wife; he was quite indifferent to the storm of anger Philippe Auguste of France loosed on John's head at this blow to French influence in Syria. John was old; why should Frederick not take over the government at once? The Crusade appeared opportune.

By May Frederick had tired of Ravenna and he and his vassals and their cumbersome elaborate retinues moved to Forlì, determined to force the Lombards to open the passes. Ludwig's chaplain gives details of floods, ambushes, inimical populations, and quarrelsome innkeepers; the negotiations, too, were so drawn out that the Emperor had to stop first in Parma, and then in Borgo San Donino. There Ludwig managed to obtain the desired ratification of his succession to the Misnia and Lusatian territories in the event of his nephew's death, and also considerable assistance for the Prussian campaign. Frederick also commissioned him to persuade his uncle, the Duke of Bavaria, to take over the regency of the young King Heinrich in Germany during the Emperor's absence. Ludwig, therefore, left Borgo San Donino for home, staying with his uncle on the way, and it took a good fortnight to persuade the Duke into consenting to the regency plan; that he did so was another feather in Ludwig's diplomatic cap.

Would it have been possible to spend those months of 1226 in Italy in Ludwig's position and not hear of the grievous illness of Brother Francis, whose life by then was being despaired of? The sad news he carried back to the Wartburg and Eisenach was followed only a few months later by that of Francis' death. If Elizabeth had really received that old cloak — and it is quite likely — it had become an immeasurably precious relic.

After the jubilant homecoming in August Ludwig and Elizabeth were both at Würzburg in November for an important meeting of the German princes, who were becoming very concerned over the increasing independence of spirit in the German cities. In March of 1227 the Landgraf and Landgräfin set out again for Aix-la-Chapelle where King Heinrich's young bride, Margaret of Austria, was crowned by the Archbishop of Cologne with great festivities.

On all such occasions Elizabeth found herself up against the food difficulty; one day the only thing she could eat with a clear conscience was a dry loaf which she soaked in hot water. Isentrude tells us of the murmuring behind her back, and even to her face at "this extraordinary and novel way of living." The criticism was inevitable; what she did in the Wartburg was, after all, her husband's affair; but here she was tacitly though openly challenging the whole structure of German feudal society, in a moment when such a challenge was highly irritating. Naturally the German nobles did not like it. What did she, a bit of a girl from Hungary, know of these matters that she should dare to set herself against long established custom? They probably put most of the blame on her confessor, and talked of her husband as a fool to allow it.

After the gathering at Aix-la-Chapelle Ludwig was again away, first of all helping the monks of Reinhardsbrunn against an aggressive neighbor and then in Bohemia attempting to reconcile King Otokar and Duke Leopold of Austria.

The great question of the day, however, was the Crusade which was to precede the invasion of Prussia. The former Ludwig, called the Pious, had died during the Crusade of Barbarossa; it was a family tradition that the reigning Landgraf should take the cross, and at that time preachers were insisting that wherever there were two men in a family it was the duty of one to volunteer when the Holy Places were in need. The response was considerable, for the appeal was not only to the idealist and the pious, but to the adventurous and the commercially minded who had heard that substantial earthly advantages might easily be come by in addition to the spiritual.

When the Emperor originally settled 1225 for the start Ludwig received 4000 silver marks for his armament expenses, but the sum was increased to 5000 with free shipping transport. Hermann of Salza had been commissioned by Frederick to rouse the German princes, and the Pope sent a legate to help him; ten other princes joined the expedition, and at last the preparations were really speeded up.

Early in 1227 Ludwig had taken the cross secretly from the Bishop of Hildesheim not wishing Elizabeth to know how soon they would be parted, especially as she was expecting her third baby. She would have been the first to encourage him, and yet, perhaps she had been hoping against hope that something might still further delay the Emperor. Thierry of Apolda tells us that one evening she found the Crusader's cross in Ludwig's pouch and then she understood that the time was close at hand. She fell to the ground, but "Ludwig consoled her with many gentle words."

During that spring he had a Passion play performed in the Wartburg and Caesar of Heisterbach says that eyewitnesses described it to him. The scenes were enacted entirely by clerics and represented the Betrayal, the Passion, and our Lord's death. Such a distinct Passion play was then something of a novelty, as the earliest liturgical dramas had concentrated on the visit to the sepulcher of the Marys and the entombment, in which our Lord's body was represented by a cross or even by the Blessed Sacrament reserved in a special place. There is drama in every line of the liturgy of the Passion and the human note is at its deepest and highest in the Blessed Virgin's presence beneath the cross. It was only natural that the first extra-liturgical scene should have been the singing and enacting of a *Lament of Our Lady*. All over Europe such *Laments* were composed as the spontaneous overflowing of tender devotion which had gathered impetus first with Saint Bernard and then with Saint Francis. The *Lament* could be a monologue or dialogue between the Blessed Virgin and her dying Son; it might be in Latin or in the vernacular. Two of the most beautiful were written by Francis' follower Jacopone da Todi, to whom are due the *Stabat Mater* and the *Donna del Paradiso*. The first is a liturgical Sequence but the latter is an intensely emotional and dramatic dialogue and was certainly intended to be sung and acted.

Caesar of Heisterbach tells of two performances of the Wartburg Passion play and says that the audience felt they were assisting at the very Passion of our Lord, which was indeed the object of these plays. On this particular occasion the emotional note was heightened by the knowledge that some of those sitting in the audience would soon be starting for Palestine. Who could remain indifferent when the Holy Places were still in infidel hands, or not be moved at the cry of Jerusalem, *"qui plainte et pleure pour le secours qui trop demeure"*? The Crusade was the crowning glory of the Christian Knight, ensuring his eternal salvation. Elizabeth would not have kept Ludwig from it even had she been able; of course he must go, and it had always been taken for granted that when the Emperor was ready Ludwig would accompany him. But . . . the date was drawing so close, and the badge sewn on to Ludwig's surcoat was also being engraved on every fiber of Elizabeth's being. To be parted for so long from Ludwig was the one, all-pervading sacrifice, and everything human in her cried out against it.

This time Ludwig made minute preparations regarding the government during his absence. An addition to Thierry's *Life of Ludwig* says that he wished the unborn child to be brought up in the Premonstratensian monastery of Rumersdorf if a boy, and by nuns of the same order if a girl. His brother, Heinrich Raspe, would act as regent for Ludwig's son and heir Hermann; the choice of priests for the various benefices controlled by the Landgraf was left to Conrad of Marburg whose opinion was that "the appointment of an unworthy priest was worse than the slaying of sixty men." Ludwig then summoned his vassals to Kreuzburg, and after exhorting them to keep the peace and administer justice he concluded by recalling his father's times, his valor and courage and renown, and the wars he had to wage whereas he, Ludwig, by divine grace had been able to see his land in peace. "Now for love of God and the Christian faith I am leaving these great goods, the honors and dignities that are mine, and my beloved brothers. I am leaving the wife and children who are so dear to me, all whom I love, and all the consolations of this world in order to cross the sea as a pilgrim. Pray to God that it may be His holy will to bring me back safe and sound to my lands, and that all of you may thereby be consoled. I commend to God myself, my lands and my peoples."

Probably all Crusaders were expected to make a farewell speech of this kind, and in Ludwig's case his words were sincere. He went the round of all the monasteries in his dominions to ask for their blessing and prayers, and at Reinhardsbrunn, his favorite sanctuary, the scene has been vividly recorded: Ludwig arrived there in the evening for Compline, and when the Office was ended he went and stood beside the monk who offered holy water to all the other monks as they filed out of the church. Ludwig greeted each one singly, and when it came to the turn of the abbey scholars he took the smaller ones into his arms kissing each affectionately.

The Crusaders from the Wartburg and the Eisenach district with their retinues went to meet the rest of the Thuringian contingent at Smalkald. Ludwig's whole family were there, and again he commended Elizabeth and the children to his brother's care. It was a great gathering both of nobles and followers, whose names evoke many a page of the Manesse codex and other German chronicles. Ludwig von Wartberg, Burchard von Brandenburg, Meinhard von Mühlberg, Heinrich von Stahlberg, Hartmann von Heldrungen, Rudolf von Vargila, the long roll call showed how generously the Emperor's appeal had been answered. There were those responsible for the administrative organization of the expedition, lawyers, secretaries, chaplains, among whom was Berthold, Ludwig's future biographer; probably, too, Walther von der Vogelweide whose voice reaches us in a lovely *Palästinerlied*. Walther had found that life's "true worth at last beginneth" when his lifelong prayer was answered, and he stood on the earth trodden by our Lord.

It must have been a staggering task to get even a contingent of the Crusading army under way; besides the actual combatants a whole crowd of pilgrims went too, and what an encumbrance they must have been, joining in wherever they felt inclined, Bishop Siegfried of Augsburg among them. Many families could recall the departures of their forebears and relations who had gone out to fight and pray knowing absolutely nothing of the conditions they were likely to meet, with no idea either of geography, language, or climate. Even so some had got there and come home to tell the tale and bring with them precious relics of earth from Bethlehem or water of the Jordan with descriptions of what they had seen.

At Smalkald the infantry, the cavalry, the ponderous camp equipment and a certain amount of commissariat, horse- and mule-drawn wagons were waiting to start. At last those who were going were detached from the general din and excited confusion, and among them there was no finer figure than the young Landgraf, so full of vitality, health, and strength, so handsome, every inch a Prince to be proud of. The chronicle says that he kissed his mother and each of his family in silence, the last prayers were said, the last blessings given, Ludwig was already on his horse with Elizabeth beside him, for she had begged to be allowed to go just one stage of the way. Banners were flying, trumpets sounding, laboriously to the sound of the Crusading songs taken up by the crowd the long convoy lumbered off; the glorious Crusade had started.

It was the eve of Saint John; everywhere the bonfires for the summer solstice were being lighted with immemorial customs and traditions. There would be dancing that night in all the villages and farms. Those returning home from Smalkald along roads scented with newly cut hay told each other that Saint John would protect the Crusaders; it was a proud moment when one of a family took the cross, but — Palestine was far away, and it would be a very long time before there could be any hope of a return.

Even the next day Elizabeth would not turn back, unheeding fatigue, but when the Thuringian border was reached Rudolph of Vargila suggested to Ludwig that she had come far enough. "The time has come, my Lord, for our gracious Lady to go back since thus it has to be." The saying that parting has in it something of death has never been more true than it was that day for Elizabeth. "Woe to me, miserable woman," are her only recorded words. Ludwig had taken from his pouch a ring with a sapphire engraved with an Agnus Dei which he used to seal important documents. He showed it to Elizabeth saying that she must believe any message brought her by the bearer of the ring, but another tradition says that he gave her the ring, which is how the scene is represented on the Marburg reliquary. "May God in Heaven bless and keep thee, dearly loved sister. May He bless the child thou art carrying, thou wilt dispose of it as we have promised." That day Elizabeth also took the cross.

When she reached the Wartburg she put away her court clothes, and again put on widow's dress: "Henceforth she knew no joy; she commended herself completely to God's care in solitude and sadness, and continued to increase constantly in virtue and sanctity."

Ludwig had ridden off in the full tide of hope, power, honor, riches, health, and earthly happiness; life had given him much, and promised more. He was high in the Emperor's favor — what might they not accomplish together? Frederick was awaiting his German troops in Italy and the Thuringian army made a brave show. The traveling pace could not be forced, and all along the road they were joined by other contingents and pilgrims. On they went through Franconia, Swabia, Bavaria, over the Brenner pass and thence down the Adige valley into Italy, and into the heat of an Italian summer; then the road lay through Lombardy and down the Adriatic past Ravenna where Ludwig had hunted with Frederick only a year ago. In Apulia they struck inland and Frederick came in person to meet his German Crusaders at Troia on August 3. After a three days' rest they proceeded to Melfi, an imperial stronghold, to await other reinforcements and also because an epidemic among the shipbuilders had delayed the preparations of the fleet. The Feast of the Assumption was spent in Monopoli and finally they reached Brindisi. Here despite all precautions the food ran short; apparently no one had expected so large a force. Camping conditions were bad, the northerners could not stand the heat, and all minor discomforts were aggravated by a bad epidemic of fever. There were many deaths, and part of the army melted away.

Against his doctor's advice the Emperor went to Bari to supervise the embarcation, and he took Ludwig with him even though the latter was not well. They went to the little island of Sant' Andrea at the entrance of the port, where Ludwig was taken ill with fever. However, determined as he was to carry on, they sailed away again on August 9 and came next day

to Otranto, where they took leave of the fifteen-year-old
Empress Isabelle. After paying her his respects Ludwig had
difficulty in getting back to the ship, and he looked so ill that
it was later rumored that he had been poisoned during the visit.
Realizing how grave his condition was he called for a priest;
the Patriarch Gerold of Jerusalem and Bishop Leo of Brancaleo
administered Extreme Unction and the Viaticum which Ludwig
received "with extreme devotion." Berthold never left him and
reported that he said: "Do you see all those white doves? I
shall go at the same moment as they do." These were his last
words; it was the Feast of SS. Protase and Hyacinth,
September 11.

Less than three weeks later, on September 29, Elizabeth's
little daughter Gertrude was born.

Those of the Thuringian nobles who had already sailed were
overtaken and told the news; they returned to Otranto where
the funeral was held with great ceremony and Ludwig's body
was wrapped in two linen cloths dipped in wax. After the
solemn Requiem they went sadly on their way to Palestine in
fulfillment of their vow. Ludwig was 27 and he had ruled
Thuringia for 11 years.

Would history have been different had Ludwig lived? He
was an able man, and one cannot help wondering whether he
would have managed to bring the new Pope, Gregory IX, and
Frederick to an understanding. Gregory did not believe in
Frederick's sincerity — was he not more than halfway to being
a heretic and an active supporter of Islam? On September 29
the Pope excommunicated the Emperor and disavowed his
Crusade. What would Ludwig's attitude have been? He was
spared the dilemma and the whole of the subsequent disastrous
tangle which did such harm to both Church and State.

The messengers who set out to carry the news to Thuringia
would have reached home late in November; there was mourning all through the German lands. The news was broken to
the Landgräfin Sophie, to Ludwig's two brothers, Heinrich

Raspe and Conrad, and to Guda and Isentrude. The Landgräfin Sophie, who was evidently living in the monastery, undertook to tell Elizabeth; she went to the Wartburg, and "when they were seated" in Elizabeth's apartment the older woman said: "Dearest daughter, do not be too afflicted by what the divine will has permitted to happen to my dear son, your husband." The chronicle continues: "Elizabeth thought that her husband was a prisoner not suspecting that he was dead." "If my dear brother is a prisoner with God's help and the wise counsel of friends he can be freed." Hope would not let her suspect anything else. "Dearest daughter, he is dead." The words had to be said.

Through Thierry of Apolda Elizabeth's voice reaches us: *"Tot; tot sal mir nu alle wertliche froide unde ere si."*

She got up and started to run hither and thither through the rooms "crying like one mad." No one, nothing could calm her; on she went, anything to fly from the scourge of truth. "Not this, not this." At last she fell against a wall, and the others then tried to lift her up.

Our Lord shed tears over Lazarus. "My heart was black with grief," said Saint Augustine at his friend's deathbed, and when his mother died: "My very life was torn asunder for it had been one life made of hers and mine together." And Saint Bernard wept over his dead brother, refusing any comfort. Now we have Elizabeth overwhelmed by the death of the one person from whom she could not bear to be parted. What gratitude we owe to the human grief of our Lord and the saints.

CHAPTER V

THE WIDOW

"DEAD. Henceforth all earthly joys and honour are dead to me." Those first words of Elizabeth on hearing the news of Ludwig's death were prophetic. She had not needed to see the ring to be convinced that he was dead; perhaps the other legend is true which says that the ruby of her own bridal ring had told its own tale by cracking at the moment when he died.

There was little time for repining; Elizabeth seems to have been conscious of the gathering intensity of her life in which all the different elements were being concentrated in one choice and its fulfillment. Four crucial years lay before her during which everything in her that was purely natural, however good, had to be developed and perfected into something super-natural. These years were terrible and glorious, for in them Elizabeth's vocation to share in the cross was completed, and she became an embodiment of Francis' parable of perfect joy.

The period following immediately on Ludwig's death has been a good deal misunderstood. The popular tradition made Elizabeth appear as having been brutally driven from the Wartburg with her three children by her brothers-in-law, and almost left to starve. This opinion has been proved untenable by the patient researches of German legal and historical scholars; their findings do not detract from Elizabeth, but instead of the romantic heroine of a legend we see her in her true colors as a saint and a beautiful figure of real life.

Professor Huyskens considers that she left the Wartburg of her own accord when she became a widow and took possession of the castle of Marburg to which her marriage had entitled her. She was turned out of this by the unfriendly nobility of Hesse, some of whom went so far as to forbid anyone to help or even speak to her. Master Conrad was appointed her "defender" by the Pope to protect her against these nobles, not against Heinrich Raspe. This is an extreme opinion and I can only say that had she immediately moved to Marburg, surely one of her companions would have mentioned it; it seems more probable that she stayed on in the Wartburg for a short time, and spent some months in Eisenach before making the move to Marburg. In their statement after Elizabeth's death, Isentrude and Guda said: "After the death of her husband she was put out of the castle (*ejecta*) and from all the benefices of her dowry by some vassals of her husband, his brothers being still young." Irmingarde, who only knew Elizabeth later, declared during the cause of canonization: "After the death of her husband blessed Elizabeth was for a time deprived of benefiting from the property of her husband, and this by his brother, although it is true that the latter would have granted her maintenance (*sustentatio*)."

The texts have to be interpreted in the light of legal practice of the time, and also from what can be deduced of the characters of all concerned — from the known facts of their lives. The chief actor was Heinrich Raspe, Ludwig's eldest surviving brother, who was also regent for Elizabeth's son, the five-year-old Hermann. Did he so grossly betray his brother's trust as to turn her and the children out in midwinter with no provision of any kind? Whatever Isentrude may say, Heinrich Raspe was twenty-three, and therefore certainly could not be excused on the grounds of youth. There were still seven years before little Hermann would come of age, and during that time Heinrich Raspe was unquestioned lord and heir presumptive to all Ludwig's domains. There does not, therefore, seem to have been sufficient reason for such brutal treatment of the widow and heir. What we know of Heinrich Raspe's nature makes it all the more unlikely. He has none of Ludwig's glamour and appears as an unimaginative, meticulous administrator, drawn unwillingly into the vortex of imperial policy. When confronted with the choice of supporting the Pope or the Emperor — the choice Ludwig was spared — he sided with the Pope. Under the influence of Conrad of Marburg he joined the Crusade against the heretics; and he founded a confraternity of penitents in the church of Saint Nicholas in Eisenach which seems to have been essentially Franciscan in spirit. There is no proof that he did this as an act of reparation for his treatment of Elizabeth, and he wrote to the Pope that he and his wife Gertrude wished to turn from worldly sins and to crucify the flesh and show themselves true soldiers of God. Gregory answered by appointing a Franciscan as chaplain. This, however, all happened later when Elizabeth's example was in everybody's mouth and she was already a canonized saint. For the moment we have to try and see Heinrich Raspe as he showed himself in his dealings with Elizabeth who, in 1227, was not an official saint, but only the sister-in-law with whom he had been brought up. He and everyone else knew how united she and Ludwig had been; quite possibly he had been extremely irritated by her excessive and challenging charity, but there was still a long step between that and turning her out of the Wartburg.

According to Thuringian law the succession to a title belonged to the eldest son, but all the members of a family had a share in the property. Ludwig's three children became coproprietors with their uncles and aunts, but during their minority the power of administration lay with the regent. All coproprietors of age had to give their consent to any sale or donation, and the Landgräfin Sophie and Elizabeth are mentioned on an equal footing with equal rights. The dowries of princesses who had married into the family formed part of the patrimony belonging to all; and each one received the revenues of her own dowry, generally in the form of maintenance inside the family circle. From the moment of her husband's death a widow ceased to be a coproprietor but she received maintenance and whatever jewels and precious objects she happened to possess.

Legally Elizabeth's dowry fell under Thuringian law; she had brought with her 1000 silver marks and jewels and gold and silver objects of such value that everyone had been amazed and delighted. In the marriage contract her husband had settled on her certain lands with their revenues for her life probably in the form of a "morgengab," a *"donatio propter nuptias"*; it was usual for the husband to continue to administer such property, but sometimes the wife did it herself. Neither her age nor inclination would have made Elizabeth anxious to be burdened with legal administration, and, as we know, Ludwig gave her practically a free hand with whatever she wanted for charity.

The greater part of her revenues must have come from the products of her lands passing through the hands first of Ludwig's, then of Heinrich Raspe's officials in what was virtually an estate office. With Elizabeth's recent activity during the famine fresh in their minds, the officials may have seized the opportunity for holding back her income, and Heinrich Raspe may have approved of their action. This was the moment to make good the deficiencies caused by her exaggerated and willful extravagance. Obviously Isentrude thought this to be at the root of the trouble.

What Heinrich Raspe offered Elizabeth was her maintenance (*sustentatio*); how calculating it must have seemed to Elizabeth, who in the dire grief of the first weeks of her widowhood probably took for granted that everything would go on as heretofore, and that Heinrich Raspe would continue along the same lines as Ludwig.

This was not the case: the two brothers were different characters. Heinrich Raspe was a cold nature with no imagination. He was quite incapable of understanding Elizabeth, who at that moment had nothing like the ascendancy over her brother-in-law that she had had over her husband.

She was offered her legal maintenance, and this meant that she must eat whatever was served at the family table. Ludwig had tolerated her ridiculous scruples but they had been the cause of enough criticism and gibes. It is quite likely that Heinrich Raspe and Conrad had suffered from the ill-concealed amusement and annoyance of relations and friends on this very point. Anyhow, things would be different in future.

This was the great stumbling block dividing Elizabeth from the family, as Irmingarde said later: "Blessed Elizabeth could, it is true, have been maintained in her position with her husband's brother, but she would not accept as food what had been stolen and extorted from the poor, such as is often the custom in the courts of princes."

Conrad of Marburg's prohibition was still in force, and very soon after Ludwig's death Elizabeth was faced with a predicament compelling her to come to a decision. Either she must eat what Master Conrad had forbidden or she must go hungry.

Heinrich Raspe was responsible in so far as he allowed the decision to be forced on her. It was very unkind to put her in such a position at that moment when, for one thing, she had a baby a few months old. Heinrich Raspe was legally within his rights, but he showed himself obtusely uncomprehending of the values by which Elizabeth lived and this made him indifferent to the suffering he was causing.

Elizabeth was driven to demand the division of possessions; she wanted to dispose of what was hers and evidently she had not grasped her own legal position. What did she care about the law? The proof of this came rather later when she gave the Marburg hospital to the Knights of Saint John, not consider-

ing that it was built on land over which she had no control
and could not give away. It belonged in reality to Heinrich
Raspe and his brother Conrad, having been left them by
Ludwig; and even while they were pushing the cause of
Elizabeth's canonization, they also asked the Pope to arrange for
the return of their land, alleging that Elizabeth had either been
badly advised or had acted in her own simplicity and ignorance.

As regards the things of this world Elizabeth was content
to be extremely simple; she had never been able to understand
business as did her mother-in-law and the rest of the family and
court. This had always been a barrier between her and them,
but Ludwig had protected her. Now, however, she was alone.
The lands she asked for were her marriage portion; she only
wanted to help the poor, was not this more important than
the law and the family inheritance? Anyhow they were all quite
rich enough; and she stiffened in her position. Heinrich Raspe,
backed by legal advisers, no doubt spoke of the necessity of
protecting the property for Elizabeth's children and he too
stiffened, but the misery was Elizabeth's. She had lost Ludwig,
she had no money to give away, legal discussions and documents
took the place of Ludwig's kind understanding, and at every
meal she was asked to eat what was against her conscience.
She was alone against them all, and every day her determination
grew that she would live in the way of penance which was
that of Francis, and live too for the poor.

Even Master Conrad was away at the time and Brother
Rüdiger was in Erfurt; it is said that her friends sent to tell
him of her plight and his answer was to send her a copy of
the parable of perfect joy; if so it was a prophetic inspiration.

Guda and Isentrude give us no clue of whether they tried
to influence Elizabeth's decision; they were her faithful followers
and she had the comfort of knowing she could depend on
them. No one was asking her to leave the castle in so many
words, but every day it was being made more impossible for
her to stay. The choice may have been forced by many subtle,

even unconscious means, a word here, a look there, a sudden impatience and the total incomprehension even of the pious for the one human being who was being called by God to something else; and this very incomprehension added to physical hunger was part of the means of her sanctification.

It was perhaps the darkest moment of Elizabeth's life; each corner of the Wartburg recalled Ludwig to her, each stone and turn spoke of the games they had played as children, of some joke, some little incident, of his courtship and their marriage and the Christian joy of their union. The Wartburg was the setting for all that had made up her life, and the home in which her love of God and of Ludwig had been born and grown to fulfillment, where now her own children were running about and playing even as she had done, and learning their prayers in the same chapel. The family who for so long had been hers were acting like strangers, and the familiar stones and rooms which she loved had no power to help her.

Perhaps Elizabeth hardly measured the sacrifice she was facing. As the mother of three children it was, as far as we can tell, even greater than that which had been asked of Francis or Clare. In her misery life was being narrowed down to the one point, either she must go against her conscience or she must leave and go who knows where. All her dread of Master Conrad rose; what would happen if she disobeyed him? That would mean disobeying God. Did Elizabeth put on Francis' cloak in the black oppression of the choice? For choose she obviously did, and Irmingarde says: "She would not eat food which was stolen and extorted from the poor, and she chose to be rejected (*elegit abjecta esse*), and to earn her bread like any paid woman through the work of her own hands."

Her action of refusing maintenance on Heinrich Raspe's terms was a direct attack on the feudal system, an active assertion that the serfs had as much right to the food they produced as those who sat at the Landgraf's table. In Elizabeth's mind this may have been a secondary point; above all she was concerned with the Gospel command to "love thy neighbor as thyself" and to fulfill to the utmost her vow of obedience to Master Conrad. In any case, it was the first stage of her final victory, the triumph of the spirit of Francis which chose poverty, trusting her own future and that of her children entirely to God. And unlike Clare, Elizabeth had not the encouragement of Francis' presence when she broke with the world.

Nothing tells us what finally precipitated her decision, but the winter storms were raging when she left, presumably in haste since no provision was made where she could go. Probably Guda and Isentrude went with her; they only say that next day her companions were there, and though she surely took the baby with her, the children seem to have remained in the castle, at least for that night.

No one could hurry down the steep frozen path, and it was already dark when Elizabeth reached Eisenach; there is no explanation why she did not stop in her own hospital, but she eventually found shelter in a shed where pigs were kept. Isentrude only says: "She went to the town and entered a poor house." It was bitterly cold, but to Elizabeth it was like the night of the Nativity, the night so loved by Francis when "Heaven and earth are made one." Heaven had opened in the stable of Bethlehem, in cold and poverty, and for the first time she was physically sharing those conditions, she was really poor, and "for the first time in the last dark months she was that night in great joy." Close by the bells of the Franciscan church sounded for Matins; exultant at her release, Elizabeth entered, and it is said that it was she who entoned the *Te Deum* and asked the friars to thank God for all her afflictions.

Next day the children were brought down, we do not know by what arrangement, and therefore Elizabeth had to find some other shelter. As we follow her story step by step we see her being forced, as it were, from one level of poverty to another. After the first night in the pig shed, she who had always been in the position of choosing her residence and of offering shelter to others had to beg for a lodging for herself, her children, and her friends.

It is not easy to reconstruct the story; there is no mention of Elizabeth having turned to the Cistercian monastery where her mother-in-law was; perhaps just because it was a family foundation she did not want to involve the nuns in her own difficulties with Heinrich Raspe and Conrad.

This is the moment when one has to think of the inhabitants of Eisenach; Elizabeth's poor could do nothing for her, and she was in need of material help. She was forced to appeal to the rich people of the town — to those who had felt the prick of her challenge and the tacit reproach of her example. For the most part they were prosperous, respectable, conventional citizens, again quite unable to keep pace with a saint. Some of the men held official positions in the Landgraf's administration, and as such can certainly not have approved of Elizabeth's ruinous and reckless charity; where would the public finances be if everyone went on as she had done? They probably considered it a mercy of God that such foolishness had been stopped; there was always a measure that must be respected, God did not ask for mad squandering, and in a well-ordered city women and children did not wander about in midwinter. They were thankful that the new Landgraf appeared to be a sensible person, and they turned a deaf ear to Elizabeth's appeal.

What did the women say at the sight of Elizabeth and the children in such a dire plight? A number of houses would certainly have had sufficient room to take them in, but that meant putting oneself in the awkward position almost of opposition to the new Landgraf. Here, indeed, was an object lesson of the result of exaggeration; Elizabeth had courted poverty and played at poverty, she had brought this on herself, and who in their senses would expose small children in such a way at such a time of year? They had always known that no good could come of princesses refusing to behave as they should, and trying to change the fashions and preach to other people. In any case the

Landgräfin only had to go home to the castle with the children, which was also what was being said in the Wartburg. Most of these women followed their husband's lead.

At last Elizabeth did find an open door, but a very inhospitable one where hearts were so cold that on leaving she thanked the walls that had sheltered them from the cold and rain: "I would gladly thank the persons in this house, but I should not know for what." The next day they all returned to the shed since no other refuge was available.

Elizabeth had left home, driven out by her conscience and the implacable impulse to poverty which in her was a divine vocation. She had no settled plan except to let God guide her day by day. She seems to have counted on some sort of hospitality in Eisenach which was not forthcoming. Even she saw that the children could not remain in the shed, and one feels how vividly Isentrude relived those days, how acutely she still resented the treatment of her beloved mistress when she later described what had happened: "Thus persecuted for no reason by her husband's vassals, deprived of her possessions and driven by poverty, blessed Elizabeth sent her children to different far-off places where they could be cared for and brought up."

It was a cruel plight; Elizabeth had no choice but to follow the call of God, and our Lord's own words justify her: "He that loveth son or daughter more than Me is not worthy of Me. And he that taketh not up his cross and followeth Me is not worthy of Me" (Mt. 10:37). It is true that many medieval families — including Elizabeth's own — were quite ready to surrender their children, still almost babies, in the cause of an advantageous marriage, and we have seen what happened during the Children's Crusade; still it was the hardest of sacrifices, and from this time onward she only saw the children at intervals. No one seems to have suggested that they should return to the Wartburg; Herman and Sophie went to the castle of Kreuzburg, and though for the moment Gertrude remained with her mother, it was already settled that she should go to the Premonstratensian monastery of Altenberg as her father had wished.

The first days passed and the Landgräfin was still wandering about the streets of Eisenach, no doubt to the disgust of her family as well as of their vassals. She turned to the poor, "taking the food from her own mouth to give to them," but at least some joined the current against her. Picking her steps on some slippery stones over a muddy open drain, Elizabeth met an old, infirm woman whom she knew well, and indeed may have nursed. Many things may account for what happened; anyhow they met where neither could turn back, they collided and knowingly or unknowingly the old woman gave Elizabeth a push so that she toppled over into a hole full of dirty water from which she picked herself up filthy and wet, but laughing, and was next seen washing her clothes. We feel how deeply what seemed like the ingratitude of the poor had bitten into Isentrude's love, and how she resented it, but then it is always easier to accept humiliations for oneself than for a loved one. Elizabeth was long past minding such a trifle; did those whom our Lord had healed defend Him in the hour of need? He had found very little gratitude, and He had said: "They have persecuted Me, they will also persecute you. The servant is not above his Master." In that laugh of Elizabeth we hear an echo of the Gospel as well as an echo of Francis' perfect joy.

Humanly speaking it would have been more satisfactory if the poor had shown devotion and gratitude to Elizabeth, but she knew that in any work of charity it is the receiver who gives and the giver who receives. There are so many turns and unexpressed comments in human reactions: "Why should I have to accept kindness from someone, why should she have so much and be in a position to give? If I were in her place I would do much more. Let her try what it means to be poor and have to beg." Gratitude and charity have to hold hands as part of one divine gift, and by this time Elizabeth was so busy being grateful to God for His gifts of every moment that she had no time to notice the response of others to herself. This, however, does not mean that those who loved her failed to notice and to mind.

One day in the Lent of 1228 Elizabeth was kneeling in church leaning against the wall, her eyes fixed on the altar. She knelt there a long time, and when she got back to the room where she was lodging she was seized with faintness, and would have fallen had not Isentrude caught her. Guda and Isentrude hurriedly got rid of everyone else, and Elizabeth, still supported by Isentrude, remained with her eyes fixed on the window. At last she began to laugh quietly and her face was radiant. This continued for a good hour, then, shutting her eyes she began to cry; when she reopened them her face was again lit up with joy. This alternation of tears and delight lasted until Compline when suddenly she spoke: "If Thou, O Lord, wilt remain with me, I will always be Thine, and never let anything separate me from Thee." Isentrude, in whose arms she still was, ventured to ask to whom she was speaking, and after a pause Elizabeth answered: "I saw Heaven open and my dear Lord Jesus bending down to me and consoling me for all the sufferings and trials that have surrounded me. Seeing Him I rejoiced and laughed, but when He turned away His Face as though He were leaving me then I cried. Then in His compassion He turned His Face, all kindness to me and said: 'If thou willest to be with Me, I will be with thee,' so then I answered Him as I said before to thee."

Isentrude then asked what Elizabeth had seen that morning in church during the Offertory, to which she replied: "It is not well for me to reveal what I saw, but believe me I was in great joy contemplating the secret mysteries of God."

After Elizabeth's death Conrad of Marburg wrote to the Pope: "Before God I declare that I have seldom found a woman more given to contemplation." Monks and nuns repeatedly saw how her face was wonderfully illuminated when she came from prayer, and her eyes shone with the rays of the sun.

"When, as often happened she was for hours in ecstasy, after it she took no, or little food." These words at once make us think of Clare of whom her sisters recorded: "When she came from prayer her face seemed shining as the sun, and her words were of an indescribable gentleness so that her life seemed entirely celestial."

Master Conrad's precious passage sets Elizabeth among the great contemplatives. It shows that all her exterior activity was but the radiation of prayer; indeed the hours of ecstasy gave her the strength for all her other work. Elizabeth the contemplative was the spiritual sister too of Mechtilde of Magdeburg, and though there is nothing to suggest they knew each other, at that very moment Mechtilde was leading a hidden life of prayer which corroborates Elizabeth's few words. To her too our Lord said: "Give me all that is thine, and I will give thee all that is Mine," and she spoke perhaps too for Elizabeth when she said: "Of the heavenly things which God has shown me I can speak but little, not more than a honey bee can carry away on its foot from an inflowing jar." And again: "Great is the overflow of Divine Love which never stands still, but ever ceaselessly and tirelessly pours forth so that our little vessel is filled to the brim and overflows. If we do not choke the channel with self-will it continues to flow and overflow. . . . God never left me but brought me such sweetness of love, such heavenly wisdom, such unimaginable wonders that I had little use for earthly things. . . . Prayer is naught else but a yearning of the soul. It draws down the great God into the little heart, it drives the hungry soul up into the plenitude of God; it brings together these two lovers, God and the soul, in a wondrous place where they speak of love."

As I see it, Elizabeth must have been a potent influence on the wonderful Cistercian community of Helfde which a few years after her death included Saint Mechtilde of Magdeburg, Saint Mechtilde of Hackeborn, and the two saints named Gertrude. She was not called as they were to the outward form of the contemplative vocation, nor was she called to translate her mystical experience into words, but rather to express this same union with God through her life in the world. Like Francis, Elizabeth was a poet who lived her inspiration.

"If thou willest to be with Me, I will be with thee." To Elizabeth these words of our Lord were a consolation compensating all her sufferings, and that Lenten ecstasy was the corroboration not only of the way she had chosen but the promise of a divine Presence that would never fail her. More than ever a total self-donation to God through poverty and charity was as necessary to her as air. If she had had any doubt before, it disappeared.

What Isentrude does make us realize is Elizabeth's physical state during this period and after she had left the Wartburg. She seems to have been a healthy child, but she had gone through more than enough to break any constitution. She was twenty-one, possibly hardly full grown herself; she had had three children, and during the past two years very often insufficient food, and all this had been followed by the tremendous emotional crisis of Ludwig's death, and the equally tremendous spiritual crisis of the new orientation of her life.

Probably Conrad of Marburg returned to Eisenach in the early months of 1228, and the same letter he wrote later to the Pope in view of Elizabeth's canonization deals with what happened during that Lent, and supplements Isentrude's words: "After the death of her husband, she was tending to the highest perfection, and asked me how she could acquire more merit, as a recluse or in a convent or in some other state. Her mind was fixed on her desire to beg from door to door, and with many tears she implored me to consent to this." Like Francis, she wanted to make her union with poverty a complete reality with no shadow of pretense about it. It was not a new aspiration; she had thought of it ever since she heard of him, and the moment had come when she could turn it into practice. Even in the moments of her greatest love for Ludwig the other idea

had been at the back of her mind; there had been an element
of compromise in her life, and now God had taken away all
reason for compromise. "If thou willest to be with Me, I will
be with thee." Nothing else mattered except to live in the
reality of those words.

Elizabeth was not like Angela of Foligno, for she did not
thank God for her husband's death — their love had been something too holy for that; but in the new phase of her life she
had no hesitation that she must be entirely given to God. Had
there already been a convent of the Poor Clares in Germany
perhaps she would have gone to it, but God had timed Elizabeth's life before any such foundation, and therefore her vocation lay elsewhere. She wanted the lowest place, that of having
to ask for her daily bread and to be dependent on the charity
of others.

Master Conrad, however, would not countenance a life of
vagrancy; his curt refusal of her suggestion had, from his point
of view, the advantage of forcing Elizabeth to deny her own
inclination. Master Conrad may easily have heard of the scan-
dals in Italy caused by groups of beggars wandering about in
the name of Francis; from the human point of view it was
impossible to have the mother of the future Landgraf in such
a position. Elizabeth's answer rang with the conviction of vocation: "I shall do what you cannot prevent me from doing," and
on the very day of Good Friday when the altars were already
stripped she placed her hands on the altar of a chapel in her city
wherein she had established the Friars Minor, and in the presence of several brothers she renounced her family, her children,
her own will and all the pomps of the world and all those things
which our Lord in the Gospel counsels us to give up.

Conrad's statement is categorical, and it shows that Elizabeth
took this vow of complete poverty in that same chapel where
she had joined in the friars' *Te Deum;* Good Friday that year
fell on March 24. Elizabeth wished to possess nothing, but
again Conrad would not agree, and insisted that she must keep

control of her dowry in order to pay her husband's "debts," by which was probably meant regular help to certain people and institutions. The fact that this ceremony took place in the friars' chapel shows that Elizabeth had been drawn still more deeply into the Franciscan orbit.

It was during that same spring that Elizabeth's aunt, her mother's youngest sister and the abbess of Kitzingen, sent for her. Naturally she too knew all about Ludwig's death and the happenings in the Wartburg and Eisenach and perhaps she hoped that her notorious niece might find peace in the abbey. Kitzingen was an old Benedictine foundation, admirable in its way, which however was not Elizabeth's. There is no indication whether this was the occasion when the Abbess, who had heard of Elizabeth's tremendous spirit of mortification, insisted on her having a hot bath. Elizabeth took it by splashing violently in the water with her foot and then calling out: "The bath is over."

The Abbess also arranged a meeting between her brother Eckbert, Bishop of Bamberg, and their niece about whom the family was obviously anxious. The Bishop was kind and hospitable; he had heard of what had happened in the Wartburg and of the life Elizabeth had been leading in Eisenach, which naturally did not appeal to him. He does not seem to have been capable of understanding its deeper implications, nor indeed of understanding Elizabeth. He put the castle of Pottenstein at her disposal as a residence, and did his best to persuade her to consent to the plan of her marriage with Frederick II who had lately lost his wife, Isabelle de Brienne.

Elizabeth took a firm stand on her original vow of continence should she become a widow. "My faith in God is so strong and He knows that the vow of continence which I took during my husband's life came from a pure and sincere heart. Trusting in His divine mercy I know He will preserve my chastity against any human scheme or violence for I did not make this vow subject to any condition of its being pleasing to my friends, or to any other intention God might reveal toward me. I made the vow absolutely from the time of my husband's death; and if my uncle gave me to another against my will I would oppose it, in spirit and in word, and if there were no other way of escape I would secretly cut off my nose so that no one would look at the fright I should have become." This was the family spirit speaking.

Eckbert was still unconvinced; a marriage with the Emperor could not be turned down so lightly, he argued that a vow could be set aside by a Papal dispensation, and he insisted that Elizabeth should go to Pottenstein and think it over, in other words, from this world's point of view, come to her senses. Pottenstein was to be her home till she married; there must be no repetition of Eisenach. Eckbert probably approved of generous royal charity, but hardly of extravagant, unconventional young widowed princesses being free to indulge any whim; for him the choice lay between the cloister or making the most brilliant marriage in Europe. He felt as Clare's relations did when she ran away from home to follow Francis.

Pottenstein must have been like a trap to Elizabeth and Master Conrad does not seem to have helped her; he was highly esteemed in the diocese as a preacher but perhaps he did not feel like intervening between the Bishop and his own niece. There was another reason, too, for wishing Elizabeth to marry Frederick. The Emperor had been excommunicated, his deep-seated quarrel with the Pope already threatened to become a running sore both for the Church and the Empire. Married to Elizabeth, lovely, attractive, wholeheartedly pious, her influence might bring about a change in Frederick's attitude. It was a point worth considering to such a man as Bishop Eckbert who was well accustomed to the unraveling of political tangles.

To Elizabeth, however, all this was secondary; her whole life had been spent in the middle of ambition and schemes and diplomatic marriages, and that world was completely dead to her. Neither she nor her cousin Agnes cared about marrying the Emperor; both their faces were resolutely turned to the ideal of Francis and Clare, and Elizabeth entrenched herself behind her vow. Her whole self, natural as well as supernatural, made her cling to it.

The final escape from Pottenstein came from an unexpected quarter. The Thuringian Crusaders having fulfilled their vow turned west, and their first thought was to reach Otranto where Ludwig had been temporarily buried nearly a year before. They exhumed his body "and only the bones remained whiter than freshly fallen snow." These were placed in a coffer covered with a silver, jeweled cross; the coffer was loaded onto a mule's back and, accompanied by knights from Palestine, started homeward. Wherever it was necessary to pass the night the coffer was taken to the church, and Mass offered for Ludwig's soul. Each church and cathedral where his body rested received the pall which had covered the coffer during the service. About May news reached Bishop Eckbert that the procession would soon approach Bamberg, and he sent to fetch Elizabeth and with a large concourse of clergy, knights, monks, and citizens he went with her to meet the body. To the tolling of the city's bells and the chanting of the choir the procession entered the cathedral where the Emperor Henry II and his wife Saint Cunegonde lay buried.

Standing near the tombs of these royal saints who were also her and Ludwig's ancestors, Elizabeth with Isentrude and Guda saw the coffer opened and the bones of her husband. When she could speak, Berthold the chaplain reported her words: "Lord, I thank Thee for having consoled me by this long desired sight of my husband's bones. Thou knowest that though I so deeply loved him, I do not regret the sacrifice which my dear one himself offered Thee, and which I too have offered Thee. I would give the whole world to have him back, and would willingly beg my bread with him, but I take Thee to witness that against Thy Will I would not recall him to life even if I could do it at the price of a single hair. Now I commend him and myself to Thy mercy. May Thy Will be accomplished in us." How true Elizabeth was to herself; Ludwig was still her husband, their two souls were united in the will of God.

Presumably this should have convinced Eckbert that it was useless to plan any further marriage for her. Elizabeth could not have described her enduring love in stronger terms than by saying she would gladly beg with Ludwig, for now she knew from experience the meaning of real poverty.

After the ceremony Thierry of Apolda tells us that Elizabeth sat down before the cathedral and summoned Ludwig's vassals. She rose to greet them and then told them what had happened after his death. Isentrude also tells that these knights promised Bishop Eckbert to defend Elizabeth's rights, and that had they not given this assurance the Bishop would not have allowed her to leave.

Again the procession set out, this time with Elizabeth, for Thuringia, and everywhere they passed through mourning cities and villages and many people joined the procession. All his subjects had liked and admired Ludwig and been proud of the handsome high-spirited young Landgraf. At some distance from Reinhardsbrunn the monks and scholars of the Abbey were awaiting them, and when finally the abbey church was reached the Office of the Dead was sung and numerous Masses offered for Ludwig, who was laid to rest in the presence of his wife, his mother, his brothers, and a great concourse of his people.

It is difficult to follow Elizabeth during the summer of 1228; probably it was in those months that she visited Erfurt and Gotha; Ludwig had founded a hospital in the latter place in which Elizabeth would naturally have been interested, and at her request early in the following year Gregory IX recommended that the Archbishop of Mainz should allow the brothers serving in it to build a chapel and cemetery and to have their own chaplain. This may have been one of Ludwig's "debts." It is more than likely that she also went to the abbey of Andechs which had links with her mother's family and the Benedictine nuns there claim that she showed her affection for it by giving them various objects, among them her wedding gown of Sicilian damask. She may also have been in touch with her other uncle, Berthold, who had baptized her and who was the Bishop of Aquileja. He was not Franciscan in spirit and appealed to his niece for financial help; this may account for the jewels said to have belonged to Elizabeth which are now in the Museum of Cividale.

There is no clue where she was when, on seeing some exceptionally fine gilded statues in a convent chapel, she remarked: "It would be better to spend your money on your clothes and food than on your walls; you should carry these images in your hearts." When it was suggested that some particularly beautiful image should belong to her, she answered: "I do not need it for I have it in my heart." All forms of possession had become odious to her; she felt them as obstacles blocking the flow of charity. In her perhaps unconscious impulse to save time everything superfluous had to be brushed aside, and she had to go straight to the point.

Logically this would have been a likely time for her to receive the Pope's personal letter and it was in Gregory's character to wish to comfort her, for he must have been perfectly well informed of her circumstances. His ready understanding and appreciation of revolutionary young friends had already been proved in his affection for Francis and Clare: He, the great prelate and statesman, was nearing seventy; they were in their twenties, and he was always ready to help and protect them. We have already seen him urging Francis to send Elizabeth a token of his good will, and had they ever met who can doubt that Francis would have accepted her as he did Jacopa de' Settesoli whom he nicknamed "Brother Jacopa." Gregory's letter to Elizabeth has not the warm note of personal affection shown in his letters to Clare; Elizabeth is still the princess he has never seen, but the sympathetic understanding is there:

Gregory, Servant of the servants of God to his beloved daughter in Jesus Christ, the Landgräfin of Thuringia, greeting and apostolic benediction.

Experience has taught us that love is as strong and unconquerable as death. It has sometimes been thought that distance of place and the passing of time can extinguish the fire of love and weaken the glow of attachment. On the contrary, it appears that the Spirit of Truth who fills the world with the wideness of His Love, enflames the attachment of those who are separated and pierces their heart so that all that is lost through the lack of the personal contact of those who love each other is copiously compensated by the grace of spiritual union.

Our heart is deeply moved in thinking of the lowliness and holiness, the purity of heart and body wherewith thou dost desire to bear the wounds of suffering. Therefore we have scattered the good seed in thy soul that thou mayest reap therefrom an ample harvest, and through the small seed of earthly tears mayest win unending aeons of eternal joy. The beginnings of thy pious life with God's help will joyfully prosper, and this will bring joy to the angels, to thee merit, and be an example to many. We rejoice that thou, of high rank, weak sex and tender age, in the grip of a cruel fate shoulds't give proof of faith and constancy of life and glowing love. He who is the Stone once rejected by the builders and who is, however, the cornerstone of the building, He it is who has strengthened thy hand for labor and set the uncertain steps of thy youth on the rock.

Therefore daughter, hasten to follow thy divine Bridegroom wherever He leads until He brings thee into His innermost chamber. Walk gladly in the fragrance of His anointing and rejoice. "Enriched by the words of Thy lips I have trodden hard ways." No matter how hard and rough thy sufferings may be, this hardness will be flooded with the oil of gladness and joy, the crooked will be made straight, and the rough places smooth; others run uncertainly to win an earthly reward; not as a stranger and guest but as the bride of the Lord hasten thou along the road to receive thy well earned crown.

Gregory had understood that nothing would make Elizabeth remarry.

CHAPTER VI

THE SAINT

If Elizabeth returned to Eisenach it was only for a short time; her future was forged in a few sharp blows. Isentrude gives an idea of the situation when she says rather bitterly: "After the burial of her husband everyone neglected her interests, and she found herself in the same poverty as before." This must mean that when the Crusading knights got back to the Wartburg they were engulfed in the new regime and proved themselves rather broken reeds. They had become the vassals of Heinrich Raspe; they still loved and honored Elizabeth, but they saw the weak side of her position, and though she had renounced the world, they had not. They might probably have done more to protect her as they had promised her and her uncle, they might have tried to obtain for her the rights over her property which she was demanding. At all events their efforts were unavailing and Isentrude, splendidly partisan as ever, thought the less of them.

In the letter later written to the Pope by Conrad of Marburg he deals with what was happening from another point of view: "Seeing that she might be drawn back into the tumult of worldly glory in that district where she lived in honor during her hus-

band's lifetime, she followed me against my will to Marburg
situated on the frontier of her husband's possessions."

This needs to be read in conjunction with Isentrude's account
in which she states that Elizabeth went to Marburg at Master
Conrad's bidding. Critics have given various explanations of
the contradictions, and knowing Elizabeth's fear of Conrad it
seems incredible that she should have taken so grave a step in
defiance of his order. There must have been some misunder-
standing or perhaps two separate occasions and changing circumstances explain the two versions. Anyhow to Marburg
Elizabeth went.

The *Libellus* says that this pleasant little city on the Lahn
river formed part of Elizabeth's jointure; at any rate her possession of it was ratified in the agreement concluded between the
Landgraf and Master Conrad, who had been instructed by the
Pope to protect her and arrange the business of her property
with her brother-in-law. After her death Heinrich Raspe and
Conrad wrote to the Pope saying clearly that they had given
her the use of the land for her lifetime on which she could
build the hospital. Elizabeth only wanted poverty but she was
the mother of Hermann, who in another seven years' time
would be a ruling sovereign in his own right; it was not so easy
to regulate her affairs, or even to direct her. According to the
agreement Elizabeth renounced all claim to maintenance and
her name no longer would appear on official documents as one
of the family. In addition to the plots of land in Marburg and
other places she was to receive two thousand marks in ready
money, and whatever remained of the precious objects she had
brought from Hungary; a great deal had been sold during the
famine, including apparently the silver cradle. The negotiations
must have gone on for quite a period because, according to
Irmingarde, a later friend of Marburg days, Elizabeth was in
great financial straits after her arrival in Hesse.

The reaction of the Marburg nobility when they heard she
was coming was what might have been expected. By now every-

one knew exactly what she stood for, and very few people sympathized with or understood her. Perhaps Elizabeth's serene acceptance of their attitude galled them, and they retaliated by commenting on how quickly she had forgotten her husband and how cheerful she was. This indeed must have wounded her to the quick.

The natural lodging for her in Marburg was the castle, a fine medieval building to which she was legally entitled, but unless she had turned it into a hospital she would not have known what to do with it. It may have been during the first weeks that some of her critics tried to set the townspeople against her, or she may have preferred to wait somewhere else for the final settlement of the business. Anyhow she spent some months in the little village of Wehrda where she lived in a miserable hovel with Guda and Isentrude. It was very hot in summer, very cold in winter, but evidently Elizabeth found peace there for she seems to have returned several times during the next years. There was an abbey nearby and the abbess was her friend; there was also a hermit whom she sought out; perhaps like Francis she longed for the purely contemplative life and would willingly have hidden herself away from everyone.

Her work, however, lay in Marburg, where the hospital she had planned was already being built. The Franciscans had arrived there in 1225 and in their chapel she made a new, solemn profession. With her hands on the altar she again renounced her will and everything she possessed or anything God might ask of her; her hair was shorn and she received from Master Conrad the gray homespun habit, the cord, and the veil of the Franciscan Third Order. Isentrude and Guda entered the Order with her, and Guda later recorded that "thereby she made solemn attestation of the vow of chastity she too had made several years previously in the hands of Master Conrad."

This was the ratification of Elizabeth's earlier renunciation and also of her dedication to the ideal Francis had given to the outer circle of his followers, to Giacoma de' Settesoli, to

Praxedes, Lucchesio, Bonadonna, and many others. Only a few months previously Francis had been canonized amidst the jubilation of Christendom, and the mantle of his ideal fell also on Elizabeth. It was the mantle of a spirit far more than of a "rule," though the rule was necessary and for these followers it had first been drawn up by Cardinal Ugolino who based it on the rule given by Innocent III to the Umiliati. That rule is lost and a new version was published in 1228 and no doubt quickly transmitted to the friars in Germany; those who professed it were to be known as the Brothers and Sisters of the Order of Penance, and behind the cold rather legalistic clauses there shines the spirit of Francis' Letter to All Christians. Such a rule was an innovation; it was the consecration of men and women living in the world to the life of the Gospel; through it the spirit of the cloister had to be actualized under other conditions, and naturally only a few understood it. Elizabeth could truly say that such a form of life was despised by many "but if there were any other held in greater contempt then I would choose that." These early Tertiaries recited the canonical hours, and went to Confession and Communion at least three times a year though many followed Francis' own practice of far more frequent Communion; it was also decreed that they were not to indulge in feasting, dancing, and worldly pleasures; they fasted from All Saints to Easter, abstained on four days every week, dressed in clothes of poor, cheap stuff, wore no colored ribbons, no embroidered sleeves, were bound to the seven corporal works of mercy, to keep peace, not to go to law, to make their will, to pay their taxes. In all this Elizabeth had far surpassed the Rule, and indeed showed and continues to show what the Rule can be when it is inflamed by the spirit of Francis.

There was another clause which at that time was revolutionary and must have met with the same feudal and official disapproval in Germany as it did in Italy. The Brothers were not bound to take oaths or bear arms and they could not be forced into accepting any civil office. The clause was not new, for Innocent III had already given it to the Umiliati of Lombardy; but it was extremely important because it freed members of the Third Order from taking the feudal oath and therefore from the obligation of fighting for their feudal lord. The regulation was modified fairly soon, and Brothers were allowed to fight for the Church, to defend their country from invasion, and in self-defense, but the whole idea was that both Brothers and Sisters were apart from "the world" even though not enclosed. Their standard was that of the Gospel which indeed is the enduring message of Francis. Like him, Elizabeth took the Gospel literally, the evangelical counsels were true and possible of fulfillment; like him, she cared desperately about her fellow men and was convinced that the "world" as she knew it, could only be conquered by its opposite, the life and spirit set before us by our Lord in the Gospel.

Her prayer on the occasion of her taking the habit shows us what she considered her chief attachment to the things of this world: "God has heard my prayer and I consider as dirt all the goods of this world which hitherto I loved. God is my witness. I am no longer preoccupied with my children and I love them as I do my neighbor. I have confided them to God that He may do with them as He pleases. I rejoice, too, in the calumnies of those who are against me, in their scorn, and my only love is God."

Like Francis, Elizabeth could say these words with absolute truth; her self-donation to God was as perfect as his, and through it she had become a shining personification of his ideal of perfect joy. Her scale of values was that of the Sermon on the Mount, and she was completely identified with all that was contrary to "the world" in our Lord's sense of the word. To us she appears as one of those human beings set by God as an example of the sublime and also terrible vocation of self-surrender which is the essence of, and also the glory of the cross. To her all that she had given up was little in comparison to what the Son of God had renounced for her. Abraham had

not spared himself when called on to sacrifice Isaac because
his son belonged first to God and then to him; Elizabeth, too,
did not spare herself, but no one could accuse her of not having
minded, and perhaps one of her greatest victories was to rejoice
in the calumny that she was indifferent. The irony of the
criticism was that few would have raised an eyebrow had she
been ready to marry the Emperor quite soon after Ludwig's
death. The criticism sprang from a very different source; her
example had made too many people feel uncomfortable.

It did not take Elizabeth long to discover the poor and sick
in Marburg; she gave them all the material help she could and
lavished her personal care on the worst cases. Those who could
walk were invited to come and sit at her table, and when
Master Conrad remarked upon it she replied that she obtained
great graces of humility from it, and reminded him how she had
lived hitherto repeating that "extremes can only be cured by
extremes." She had that clarity of mind which saw things with
perfectly clear edges; and had come to hate power and riches
as instruments of oppression which divided men from each
other and wounded the Mystical Body of Christ. She saw the
power of riches battling against the power of love and attempting to subjugate the world; there could be no compromise between them even as our Lord admitted no compromise between His Kingdom and the "world." In every sense the Gospel
was Elizabeth's book of life; like Francis, the evangelical counsels were her law, and she found no Beatitude in which the
blessing is on riches and power. Her whole nature was concentrated in the literal following of Jesus whom she saw as the
Healer, the Friend of the poor, the suffering, and the outcast.
For her there was no choice; she had to go to extremes also
because she felt called to make reparation for the evil in the
social order to which she belonged.

In another point, too, she equaled Francis, and that was in
her idea of obedience; for her as for him it sprang from a completely sacramental view of life. Master Conrad had been set

over her by God; there must be no limit to her willing obedience to him. He realized his responsibility, but all we can say is that Master Conrad did not fulfill Francis' ideal of a superior!

In Conrad's view Elizabeth had given up a great deal, but not yet all; her two friends were still with her. They had been together since childhood and Guda and Isentrude were of one mind and heart with her, every joy and sorrow had been shared. Isentrude tells of the love of each for the other, and often this had been Elizabeth's only human comfort and defense. Precisely for this reason Master Conrad dismissed them from her service as well as all who had hitherto served her. "Master Conrad tried blessed Elizabeth's constancy in many ways, breaking her will in everything, and commanding her whatever was most painful. In order to make her suffer more, he took from her one by one those followers whom she loved so that she suffered in losing each one. Finally he dismissed me, Isentrude, whom she loved above all, and she wept many tears with great sorrow at our separation. Then, as the last, he sent away my companion Guda who had been with her since their earliest childhood and for whom she had a most particular love, and blessed Elizabeth took leave of her with many tears and sighs. Master Conrad of holy memory acted thus from just zeal, and with good intention; he feared that blessed Elizabeth should recall with us her former glory, and perhaps derive temptation and regret from this. . . . Besides this he took from her all human consolation she found in us because he wished her to belong only to God."

In these words Isentrude is perfectly fair to Master Conrad even though her own love and suffering quivers just below the surface. That she could write as she did shows how worthy she and Guda were of Elizabeth, and how their hearts too were set on God. It must have cost her and Guda a great deal to emphasize his *"bono zelo"* so consistently. Isentrude knew that Elizabeth's only human consolation was to talk to them, not so much of past glories as of Ludwig; that was now taken from

her. For the future Isentrude and Guda would only be allowed
to pay her short visits with little opportunity for talk, and with
the additional sting that Elizabeth was forbidden to offer her
friends any food.

Two faithful Hungarian retainers, David and Frakasius, had
already been sent back to Hungary.

Master Conrad replaced her friends with three attendants;
one was an unidentified man, who may have been a Franciscan
lay brother, or a certain Heinrich who was summoned later to
give evidence in the Cause of Canonization and afterward became a Franciscan Friar, but there seems to have been another
Heinrich to whom Elizabeth gave a corporal she had made and
embroidered.

The women we hear of are a rough servant girl, Elizabeth,
an austere and deaf old lady, and Irmingarde who was efficient,
and to a certain extent understanding. The first two were
supposed to report to Conrad on what Elizabeth did, and the
chief reason for their appointment seems to have been that
"she should be well exercised in patience."

As always Elizabeth went to the furthest possible point in
this experience; half measures had never been for her. When,
therefore, she had to part with her friends she set about exploit-
ing the new situation in the interests of humility. She would
not allow her companions to call her "Lady"; they were to say:
"Thou, Elizabeth"; they were to sit with her at table and eat
from her plate. Irmingarde, who was frank and direct and
surely liked by Elizabeth, burst out one day: "You will acquire
many merits through us, but you don't mind that we may
become full of pride because we eat and sit at table with you."

"All right, then you shall come and sit on my knee," was
Elizabeth's answer; nothing apparently could blight her serene
gaiety, and neither the deaf old lady nor the rather heavy
servant girl who were now in the place of her intimate friends
ever made her impatient. This, too, she had in common with
Clare who "was always gay in the Lord and never seen to be

disturbed." That dearly bought gaiety of Elizabeth's was something everyone remembered. But she knew how to reprove without a touch of complacency; for instance if she heard unkind gossip she would ask, "and where, please, is our Lord?"

Master Conrad's ingenuity in finding occasions to try her obedience never seemed to fail. Near Wehrda there was a hermit and Elizabeth found comfort in going to see him. Then one day Master Conrad overtook her and ordered her to turn back. As usual she obeyed: "Let us be like the tortoise which retires into its shelter when it rains; for the sake of obedience let us turn back from the way along which we had started." Surely, Francis would have liked the comparison with the tortoise. Whenever Conrad appeared from one of his preaching tours something of this kind was sure to happen.

What appears to us as an outrageous instance was when he once suggested she should go to Altenberg where he would decide whether or not she was to become a recluse. Hearing of her arrival the nuns asked Conrad to give her permission to enter the enclosure. "Let her do as she wills," he replied, and from these words Elizabeth concluded that she was authorized to do so, and went in. He sent for her and showed her the written words that she must obey his orders; her action was guilty. He ordered her to prostrate herself with Irmingarde, who had not even gone in but stood outside holding the key after opening the door. This, however, did not help her, and Brother Gerard, probably a Franciscan who generally accompanied Elizabeth, was ordered to scourge both her and Irmingarde with a heavy rod while Master Conrad intoned the *Miserere*.

Irmingarde, who admits no extenuating excuse for Master Conrad, recorded that she bore the marks of the rod for three months, and Elizabeth for much longer. The latter commented on the episode from another angle: "We must willingly suffer such things because then we are like a rose bush growing beside a river. When the water overflows the bush bends beneath the flood and the water passes over without breaking it; then when the flood ceases the rose bush emerges intact and well satisfied with its own joyous vigor. When sometimes we are bent down and humiliated we rise again satisfied and glad." This too is worthy of the Fioretti.

Even Master Conrad seems to have had some qualms over his treatment of Elizabeth, for in his letter to the Pope he excuses himself for having inflicted violent blows on her because she had kept a leper girl in her house against his orders. Still he never erred on the side of misgivings.

Elizabeth had reached a point where he could find no fault, no sin to correct; at the utmost she might feel some satisfaction in her vocation of charity, there might be some slight shadow of self-will left in her desire for total renunciation. So he attacked her on this point, forbidding her ever to give away more than one penny at a time. Elizabeth circumvented this by giving more often, which was countered by Master Conrad's prohibition against her giving anything but bread. Again Elizabeth used the same tactics; she could and would not consent to the poor being deprived. His final effort was to limit what she gave to pieces, not loaves of bread, but in this encounter we feel that victory lay with Elizabeth.

In all fairness we have to remember that Isentrude, who had much more perception than Irmingarde, says that Master Conrad's attitude about the almsgiving was influenced by his wish not to see Elizabeth fall back into the total destitution of Eisenach. His odious system of making her attendants spy on her had the same object in view. She could hide nothing from him and when she gave away money and clothes through a third person somehow he always heard of it and punished her with blows, even boxing her ears. "And she bore every blow and humiliation with extreme patience and joy." Again we remember the last clause of Saint Francis' description of perfect joy: "If we endure all things patiently and with gladness thinking on the sufferings of our Blessed Lord which we must bear for love of Him, O Brother Leo, write that herein is Perfect Joy. . . . Above all graces and gifts of the Holy Spirit which Christ gives His friends is the gift of overcoming oneself, and for love of Him gladly bearing pain, insults, disgrace and hardship."

One legend says that Rudolph of Vargila went to warn her that there was gossip over her relation to Conrad; indeed legends have woven many stories round the recorded facts. Rudolph was her devoted knight; his visit may quite well be true, but it seems very unlikely that Elizabeth showed him the marks of Conrad's blows on her shoulders, as the legend asserts.

Elizabeth seems to have known the kind of fear that Francis told his friends was a safeguard. A legend tells that one day Brother Rüdiger had come to see her and they were walking by the Lahn. Elizabeth told him of the fear she felt at the thought of her sins, and none of his reassuring words comforted her. "But why do my fears last?" she asked. He pointed to a tree growing on the opposite bank: "It would be far easier for that tree to jump across the river than for God to fail in generosity to one of His creatures." And instantly the tree had moved and was growing beside them. This may be a legend, but it is also an allegory.

There had to be many legends about Elizabeth if only as an attempt by her friends and followers to explain the secret of her behavior, of her being, and in a way to console themselves for the outward hardship she endured. So she is said to have been constantly consoled by visions of our Lady and the saints; when a woman ran off with her clothes an angel replaced them withholding a crown "because our Lord will soon crown thee with glory." The legends are like a lovely garland of flowers round the reality of Elizabeth's complete correspondence to the divine grace.

Like Isentrude, Irmingarde noticed that Elizabeth often cried when she was most joyous, and that the tears did not distort her face. "It seems extraordinary," she commented, "to weep and rejoice at the same time." Here Irmingarde shows inexperience; even on the natural plane tears spring both from joy and anguish and the same is true on the supernatural level where they can also be a direct gift of God, an answer to prayer. The lives of saints constantly oscillate between joy and grief, joy in the glory and all-ruling love of God, in His nearness to us, grief for our refusal of that love and the barriers sin sets up against it. To quote only examples nearest to Elizabeth: Saint Clare was often seen to cry "as though her heart were being poured out," and this did not only happen when she was meditating on the Passion, but in the joy of receiving Holy Communion. Francis is generally thought of as the saint of joy, yet in the early days of his conversion he was seen sobbing as he wandered round the Porziuncula. A passerby asked the cause of such grief, to which he replied: "I am weeping over the Passion of my Lord Jesus Christ and I will not be ashamed to weep over it until the end of time." The woods and rocks of La Verna heard his lamentations that "Love is not loved"; and very often his singing ended in tears, his jubilation was changed into compassion for Christ's sufferings, and he was rapt toward heaven. Mechtilde of Magdeburg said that "the nature of love is such that it overflows at first in sweetness, secondly it becomes rich in understanding, thirdly it abounds in desolation." Saint Gertrude, too, knew the extremes of joy and desolation, so did blessed Angela of Foligno and Julian of Norwich. Elizabeth is like them. Few of her own words have reached us but her friends noticed her frequent tears when she prayed and understood that they came from both joy and sorrow. Of others whose faces were distorted when they cried, Elizabeth once said: "It almost seems as though they wanted to frighten our Lord. We must give God what we have gladly and with joy." Elizabeth gave God all she had, keeping back nothing, and those few simple words so charged with meaning are a summary of her whole life.

Supernatural joy is harder to fathom than sorrow but it was

the secret of that gay serenity noticed by Isentrude, Irmingarde, and by all who were in contact with Elizabeth. After her first wild grief at the news of Ludwig's death, it never left her. Newman has described it:

> "That peace and joy uprising in thy soul
> Are earnest to thee of thy recompense,
> And Heaven begun."

Nothing could disturb the heaven in Elizabeth's soul, and it shone through all the daily preoccupations of real poverty. Once when she received a present of fish she sold it to provide for other needs, and her chief means of subsistence came from work. She used to spin wool for the monastery of Altenberg where little Gertrude was, but she did not know how to spin flax. She worked exceedingly hard; Irmingarde might take away the distaff to try and make her rest when she was ill, but she went on preparing the wool. Once when Master Conrad summoned her to Eisenach, probably on business, she returned the unspun wool with part of the price she had received in advance for the work. Francis wished all his followers to work — he had no use for Brother Fly — and Clare gave the same example to the Second Order, Elizabeth to the Third.

It was thus that she was found by some Hungarian envoys sent by her father and brother to find out the truth as to her condition; they had evidently been disturbed by the news from Eisenach. The Hungarians, led by Count Banfy, tried to persuade her to return to Hungary for naturally they were horrified when they found her working like any servant: "This is the first time a King's daughter has been seen spinning wool," they exclaimed, remembering the money and treasures and Elizabeth's whole worldly position. They found her surrounded neither by courtiers nor friends, but with the sick and needy and outcast; she would certainly rather have died than follow their suggestion, and the impressions they took back to Hungary must have caused consternation in her family. Perhaps, however, when her little nieces Margaret, Kunigunde, and

Julienette, heard the stories of this extraordinary aunt something awoke in them by which they would be drawn at least in the same direction.

Her whole way of life proclaimed that for the sister of Saint Francis poverty was a privilege and social distinctions no longer existed. She shared in all the menial household jobs, would clean and scrub, and often contrived to send the others away after dinner so that they should find the dirty dishes washed and put away when they returned. She always set aside the best of everything for the sick, and for herself she wanted to eat as little and as poorly as possible; she may have been haunted by the memory of banquets with everyone eating and drinking too much, anyhow she went to the opposite extreme with her habitual thoroughness. She had, however, a certain elementary prudence for she wanted to keep alive in the service of the sick to which she felt God had called her, and she did consult a doctor as to how far she could go in privations without serious damage to her health. She ate neither meat nor fish, she drank no wine, she slept on boards: the regime in San Damiano under Clare hardly went further. Her clothes were as near those of Francis as she could make them; the stuff was the cheapest possible, and when a skirt was too short, it was lengthened with a piece of a different color. She had a partiality for patches, and when we remember the various habits of Saint Francis we are all the more inclined to believe that his old cloak did reach her, and even served as a pattern.

From Irmingarde we gather that Elizabeth went again during this period to see her aunt at Kitzingen, and the line she had taken must have been just as critically and approvingly followed in the convents as in the world. Her connections with Altenberg were particularly close, and the hospital in Marburg was already functioning. It was dedicated to Saint Francis, one of the earliest foundations to bear his name, and early in 1229 Gregory IX gave a special indulgence to all who should visit and pray in it on the patron's feast, October 4.

Everything Elizabeth possessed went into the hospital which was built in the lower part of Marburg near to where the church dedicated to her would stand, built, too, in haste within not many years. She had various helpers. Hermann and his wife Irmentrude, the chaplain who was a secular priest named Crafdo, her own servants Irmingarde and the girl Elizabeth, perhaps others whose names have disappeared. The Franciscans had been established in the city since 1225, but their connection with the hospital was spiritual and not official. Legends tell of her devotion to the friars and her care of them.

She had arranged a small and very simple lodging for herself in the hospital building so as to be able to look after the patients by day and night. Her example in that hospital must have had many repercussions, and I cannot help thinking that it inspired Mechtilde's rather later description of how to behave in a monastery: "Thou shalt go daily to the sick house, and heal the sick with lovely news of God, and cheer them gently with earthly joys too for God is very rich. It is good to cherish cleanliness in the sick, to be merry and laugh with them in goodly manner, to service them eagerly and lovingly enquire into their illness and pains. If thou stand by them in this way, then will God's love flow sweetly into thine own soul." Every word fits!

She took a paralyzed child who was an orphan to sleep with her, and no trouble was too great for her in looking after him. Conrad of Marburg later wrote to the Pope that it was done as a "mortification"; it is easy to guess where the mortification lay. When the child died his place was taken by a leper girl whom Elizabeth not only nursed with the same devotion as Francis has always shown, but whom she amused and consoled and treated as a friend. She had begged her attendants not to tell Master Conrad of the girl's presence in the house, but eventually, of course, he heard of it, and the girl was sent away. Even then, however, Elizabeth made sure that she was looked after, and often went to see her.

The next person to be adopted was a child whose head was completely bald through skin trouble, and he too was nursed and cared for and mothered. All that Elizabeth had learned about the treatment of illness and her own considerable experience was put into the service of the sick, and the more miserable and repulsive the case, the more Elizabeth loved and served that person. "What a joy for us to be able to bathe and nurse and clothe our Lord," she exclaimed one day, and Irmingarde recorded her own answer: "A joy to do all this? I don't know if others agree with you." Elizabeth might have pointed out that it was not a question of agreeing with her but with our Lord. His presence might be hidden, but to her it was as real as in the Blessed Sacrament; He had said "In so much as you do it to the least of these My brethren you do it to Me"; therefore He met her in every bed, in every knock on the door, in every cry. Elizabeth's care was for both body and soul: those sick folk in the Marburg hospital were not saints but ordinary suffering human beings who probably did not want to suffer and desperately wanted to get well. These were the people with whom our Lord had identified Himself, and Elizabeth's human sympathy and gift of herself were immeasurably heightened because she knew He was there. All the sick realized how deeply she minded what happened to them, the comforting touch of her hands could alleviate pain, her gay serenity brought the sun into those rooms, and when she spoke of Jesus those who listened wanted to hear more. Her spiritual touch was light and deft; she never asked of others more than they could give knowing that the crumbs may be as valuable to God as the loaves, and therefore to be eagerly saved and if possible increased. There was no pedantry about Elizabeth even when she was insisting that the patients should go to Confession and Holy Communion, and one very drunken old woman even got a beating.

There was no doubt that Elizabeth was as incapable of keeping money as Francis. Almost as soon as she received the money of her dowry and her remaining jewelry she started to sell the latter and decided to distribute five hundred marks — a very large sum in those days — on one day. She sent out messengers to the places within twelve miles and naturally she collected a crowd. Like Francis Elizabeth never attempted to distinguish between the worthy and unworthy; she only wanted to give. However, on this occasion she ordered everyone to sit down in rows, and no one was allowed to move for she had no intention of letting the more astute hold out their hand twice; anyone found cheating had a lock of hair cut off. A girl named Hildegunde was caught, and she had magnificent hair; she was taken crying to Elizabeth and her hair was cut off. At last someone came forward and explained that it had all been a mistake, and Hildegunde was not among the beneficiaries but was only looking for a relation. "At any rate," said Elizabeth, "now she won't be able to go dancing." She called the weeping Hildegunde and asked whether she had never thought of serving God more thoroughly, and Hildegunde confessed that for a long time she had wanted to become a nun but could not bring herself to it on account of her beautiful hair. "I am more glad that you have lost that hair than I should be had my son become emperor," was Elizabeth's rejoinder. And this would have been a real possibility had Elizabeth herself preferred marriage with the Emperor to the service of God.

Hildegunde remained with Elizabeth as a servant in the Marburg hospital. She told her story on oath during the ecclesiastical inquiry preceding Elizabeth's canonization. The beautiful cut off hair had been kept and was shown to the commission.

By nightfall most of Elizabeth's guests had gone, leaving the oldest and weakest and poorest who were preparing to sleep in the courtyard. Just because they were so needy Elizabeth insisted on giving them each another six Cologne pennies and any children received the same. Then they were provided with supper: "Let us make them really contented," said Elizabeth, and she ordered fires to be lit. After this she made the round, washing and binding up painful feet, and when the guests began to sing she turned to her companions: "I told you we had to make them happy." It was worth any effort if someone could be made less miserable even for a few minutes: "and she herself rejoiced with those who were glad."

In all Elizabeth's giving there was a smile, and we seem to see the reason why God had given her such gaiety as it were in return for all her sufferings, poverty, and renunciation. She was the channel by which it had to reach others and the smile was never withheld. As in Eisenach she was soon a familiar figure going in and out of the poorest houses of Marburg, paying great attention to the clothing and beds of those she visited, always carrying her gifts "with her own hands." Besides the work in the hospital she found time to get to know everyone who was in need.

Evidently she still went sometimes to Wehrda, and on one occasion a homeless woman about to have a baby knocked at the door. She was taken in and the baby received the name of Elizabeth. A month later the woman wished to leave and was given clothes for herself and her husband, food, money and Elizabeth's own shoes while her fur sleeves were cut up to make a warm wrap for the baby. While Elizabeth was in church for Matins she remembered something else and told her servant, the other Elizabeth: "Go and look in my purse and give what money there is to that poor woman, who may need it." The maid returned saying that the woman had gone leaving the baby behind.

A woman was found to take the child and then at Elizabeth's request the civil guards sent out messengers to look for the mother. She could not be found and the servant suggested that Elizabeth should ask God for the discovery of her whereabouts: "I can only ask God that His will may be accomplished." In this short answer Elizabeth recorded the heart of her own spiritual life. Not long afterward the baby's father arrived, saying that he had been impelled to come by an overwhelming impulse; he told where his wife was and she was brought back. In shame she asked Elizabeth's forgiveness and someone suggested that the things she had received should be taken back and given to another poor person. Elizabeth only said: "Do whatever seems to you most just"; but after the things had been given to others the woman was not the loser, for Elizabeth provided for her again as soon as she had taken back the baby.

Another incident that happened at Wehrda is of particular interest for it shows that at least some of the local nobility had been won over to Elizabeth. A lady, Gertrude von Lembach, came one day to see her bringing with her an elegant young man Berthold, her son.

Elizabeth turned to him: "Why don't you serve the Lord, your Creator?"

"O, my Lady, do pray that He may give me the grace to serve Him."

She agreed to do so, insisting that he should pray with her in order to prepare himself for the grace he desired. She fell on her knees, and as usual was lost to all outward things, noticing nothing of what was going on. At last Berthold cried out: "O, my Lady, please stop praying," and his mother and the servants saw that his whole body was shaking and his clothes were wet with sweat. "In God's name, stop," he cried, "this fire is burning me up." He was so hot that those near him could hardly bear to touch him. This happened in the year before Elizabeth's death, and Berthold became a Friar Minor.

The year 1231 saw Elizabeth hard at work, unsparing with herself, entirely dedicated to the increasing demands of the hospital and the poor. She seemed well; so well indeed that Master Conrad, who was ailing, asked her how she would order her life after his death. She told him calmly that she would be the first to die, adding that she was already close to death.

Four days later she fell ill, and after twelve days had passed she asked that her room should be cleared of all outsiders, for many people including nobles had crowded to see her. The only exception she made was the beggar child with scurvy whom she had nursed back to health. She kept him sitting beside her. As an excuse for wishing to be alone she said that she "wanted to meditate on God's judgment and His almighty power."

The Feast of Saint Martin, a saint greatly revered and loved during the Middle Ages, came and went. On the following Sunday, November 16, Master Conrad heard her confession but afterward told that she had said nothing beyond accusing herself of faults she had mentioned previously. He asked her what was to be done with her belongings after her death, and she answered that anything she might own was the property of the poor. She expressed the wish to be buried in the poor habit and cloak she habitually wore. She received Holy Communion, and all that day repeated words of sermons that had appealed to her, dwelling especially on the raising of Lazarus and on our Lord's tears at his grave.

When she saw that those standing round were crying she said: "Daughters of Jerusalem, weep not for me but for yourselves"; after this she turned to the wall and was silent. Then those present heard her voice coming very softly though her lips did not move. They asked whence the voice was coming, and after a little Elizabeth replied inquiring whether they had not heard "those who were singing with me"? She turned round to Elizabeth the servant, "Where are you, my dear?"; and the maid answered: "I am here"; adding "O my Lady, how sweetly you were singing." "Did you hear?" said Elizabeth. "Between me and the wall a bird was singing so beautifully and its voice made me sing too." All that evening she remained in a state of joy and peace. Then a cloud seemed to come over her and she asked anxiously: "What should we do if the devil appeared?" Then louder she cried out: "Go away, go away; go away." The dark moment passed; her voice sank; "Let us talk of God and of the Child Jesus, for it is now about the time He was born and lay in the manger, and created a new star no one had ever seen before." She was very weak but said she did not suffer. She commended all about her to God saying to Irmingarde: "This is the moment when almighty God calls His friends to Himself." She died as though falling asleep a little after midnight between November 16 and 17.

She was buried in the church of the hospital on November 19, and all the countryside flocked to see her lying as it seemed asleep, with a fragrance in the air that seemed to convey a mysterious sense of comfort. The Cistercians and other religious orders were there; everyone wanted a bit of her poor gray habit, a relic, for there was no doubt in any mind that the little figure lying before them was a very great saint. Her friend, the abbess of Wetter, heard the singing of multitudes of birds, and when she went outside to look, there they were sure enough singing for Elizabeth, as those of the Porziuncula had sung for Francis.

CHAPTER VII

THE GLORY

IT COULD be truly said of Elizabeth that in her end was her beginning. Her triumph was already born during her earthly life to be completed afterward. Many of the poor and sick had early recognized her for what she was; her own feudal world, almost from force of circumstance, was slower of comprehension. When, however, the earthly existence of the brilliant, challenging young woman suddenly ended all eyes were opened before the inconfutable proof of her life and the ensuing miracles. It was generally admitted that here was a human being with totally different values from those of most people; someone to whom the thought "me first" was unknown. God was always first in everything for Elizabeth, then came those she felt called to serve, and lastly "me."

To be left without Elizabeth must have been an appalling outlook for the inconsolable hospital patients and the needy and sick folk of Marburg. Then, the very day after the funeral a Cistercian monk who had been out of his mind for forty years suddenly recovered as he was praying at her tomb. It was the sign that their Elizabeth had not forsaken them; she was still among them with increased power to help and heal. The news

ran like wild fire, all the sick who could move or be carried set
out for Marburg, jolting along vile roads in any weather, sure
that Elizabeth was waiting for them, and would continue from
heaven to do good on earth. It was the medieval counterpart to
Saint Thérèse of Lisieux. And sure enough the blind obtained
sight, the lame walked, the deaf heard, dreadful diseases were
instantly cured, the mad recovered their reason.

Master Conrad was there taking careful note of what happened, and soon at the request of the Pope's penitentiary,
Brother Raymond of Penafort, he was preparing to send
details to Rome, for no one doubted that Elizabeth would be
officially proclaimed a saint. Almost at once Master Conrad
also became the moving spirit in the construction of a new
church in place of the hospital chapel which was quite insufficient to hold the crowds flocking to Elizabeth's tomb. In August
of 1232 Archbishop Siegfried of Mainz consecrated two altars
in this new church in the presence of everyone who could
possibly get there. A document was drawn up with details of
sixty of the more striking miracles, and to this Conrad added
a long letter giving his view of Elizabeth's sanctity. The Pope
answered by commissioning the Archbishop of Mainz, the abbot
Raymond of Eberbach, and Conrad of Marburg to send a full
official report and it seemed as though the canonization of
Elizabeth would be almost as speedy as that of Saint Anthony
of Padua who had died a few months before her, and was
canonized the following year.

Abbot Raymond brought with him to Marburg an assessor,
Brother Wilhelm, who for two years had suffered from a very
bad infection in his leg. He complained repeatedly that it was
Elizabeth's duty to cure him, that indeed unless she did so he
would record no more miracles. On arriving in Marburg the
Abbot, too, prayed earnestly for his Brother, and in three weeks
the cure was complete. Brother Wilhelm was a witness in the
final inquiry held in 1235.

The report was completed in the early weeks of 1233 and at

the same time the Archbishop and Master Conrad sent another joint and incriminating account of the activity of the heretical sects of Germany. Even when he was eagerly forwarding Elizabeth's canonization Master Conrad was pursuing the heretics with his customary zeal. He never could let anything rest if it appeared to be contrary to the glory of God. He was the chief mover in the case against Graf Heinrich von Sayn and other nobles of Hesse, all powerful people who had no intention of being beaten by Conrad. They too appealed to Rome and at last Gregory seems to have realized the intricacy of the situation in Germany, and to have been put on his guard against Conrad's excessive zeal, which did not hesitate to bring forward false witnesses, or at any rate did not make sure that the witnesses were disinterested. Meanwhile Conrad insisted that the Archbishop of Mainz should summon Heinrich of Sayn to appear before a Synod in July, 1233. Count Heinrich was able to clear himself, but even then Master Conrad would not drop his accusation and the other nobles involved were men against whom he had even tried to preach a Crusade. The Synod went against him, and King Heinrich, who had been present, offered him an escort for his journey back to Marburg. Conrad refused it and set out with a Franciscan Brother Gerard Lützelkolb; between Mainz and Giessen they were attacked and killed, and the bodies were taken to Marburg and buried close to the tomb of Elizabeth. Conrad was not widely regretted, but it is only fair to say that a few pilgrims invoked his name with Elizabeth's, perhaps because he was buried nearby.

The Letter and the document concerning Elizabeth and the miracles were in the Pope's hands at the time of Conrad's death, but something delayed the Cause, which was not taken up again until 1234. The Landgraf Conrad went himself to see Gregory at Rieti in the summer of that year; his chief object was to hasten his sister-in-law's canonization, for Conrad was one of her earliest conquests; he went also in the name of his brother and was supported by Hermann von Salza who had behind him all the authority of the Teutonic Order. Both Heinrich Raspe and Conrad were anxious to insure the future of the Marburg hospital by transferring it to the Order, to which the Pope agreed. The arrangement was ratified on July 1 and Gregory also gave the Order the patronage of the parish church. On November 18, three years after Elizabeth's death, the Landgraf Conrad entered the Order with two priests and nine other knights. Gregory IX alludes to this in his Letter to Queen Beatrice of Castille, Elizabeth's niece.

In October of 1234 he ordered a new commission consisting of Bishop Conrad of Hildesheim, and the abbots Hermann of Georgenthal and Ludwig of Hersfeld to send the findings of the previous commission authenticated with their own seals to Rome within five months. The commissioners set to work on January 1, 1235, and collected the evidence of those who attributed their recovery from illness to Elizabeth's intercession, and also took down the account of Elizabeth's life given by Guda, Isentrude, and the servants of the Marburg hospital. The record of some 150 miracles has come down to us, full of human details and we almost stand by and see the painful arrival, the expectation, and hear the plea for help. Each one of these suppliants is not a case, but a person; some had known Elizabeth personally, all came with the tremendous conviction that no appeal to her could be in vain, and very many were cured. It is not surprising to know that the majority of those healed were children.

The lengthy document imploring the Pope to raise Elizabeth to the altar of the Church was signed by archbishops, bishops, abbots, prelates, dukes, and a long list of notable people, and it was conveyed by the abbot of Busch, Master Saloman, a preacher and canon of Wurzburg, and Brother Conrad of Thuringia accompanied by numerous other religious. They found the Papal court at Perugia and the documents were read to an assembly of the highest dignitaries presided over by the Pope. It was received with unanimous and admiring approval.

On May 27, the day of Pentecost, 1235, Gregory IX went in one of those processions so vividly portrayed in early Renaissance pictures to the Dominican church, and after the account of Elizabeth's life and miracles had been read with all the splendor and pageantry of the Church, Gregory pronounced the ritual formula that she was a saint in heaven. For the first time her name resounded in the *Confiteor* immediately after those of the Apostles, the collect invoking her help was read, the *Te Deum* was sung by a huge congregation, and all the bells pealed with joy in honor of the new saint. Any canonization enhances the life of the whole Church; the *Te Deum* sung on earth is part of that sung in heaven in exultation at the fulfilling of God's will through one particular soul now perfectly united to Him, and because of that not lost to earth.

On that May day Brother Conrad of Thuringia representing his Order and family gave beautifully decorated candles to the Pope and Cardinals, and candles to all present. In the name of the Franciscan Third Order he also distributed copious alms in money and food to several thousands of poor, while Gregory granted all requests made to him, and as a proof of his friendship for the Teutonic Order and for the royal house of Thuringia he also invited Brother Conrad to dine at his own table. The canonization was proclaimed in the Bull *Gloriosus in Majestate* and communicated to the bishops and heads of states. Among these the Pope's letter to Queen Beatrice of Castille is of special interest. After the usual introductory words the text continues:

In these days the Almighty has given us a *vas admirabile* which showed itself as a furnace of charity through the burning ardor of good works. This chosen vase consecrated to God is no other than Saint Elizabeth, whose name we interpret as signifying the satisfying of God since many times she nourished God in the poor and the infirm, and nourished our Lord with three loaves given her in the night of tribulation by her Divine Friend, the bread of truth, the bread of charity, and the bread of courage. In her burning love of eternal beatitude Elizabeth served the Lord of Heaven and earth with three precious dishes, she refused whatever He forbade, she obeyed each of His commands, and she accomplished all His Counsels. She subdued human desires in vigils, fasting, and prayer, thus making the creature obedient to the Creator, she subdued the senses to reason, and the flesh to the spirit. Truly of her it may be said that she is a *vas admirabile*, the work of almighty God, admirable in the virtue of humility, in the subjection of her body, in the tenderness of her compassion which will be celebrated in all ages.

Though of royal birth she made herself the servant of the poor, and sick, and until her death she was obedient to the infirm, the pilgrims and the poor. Instead of the ornaments habitual to royalty, pearls, precious stones, gold and silver, she completely threw off all worldly vanity and ambition and put on the harsh habit of poverty.

Now her brother Conrad formerly the Landgraf, still young and beloved by men and the world, has drunk of the same cup of the wine of compunction at which she drank and offered to others, for he has thrown off all worldly dignity and braving persecution has hastened naked into the shelter of the Cross whose sign he carries in his heart.

Here too is thy sister, the virgin Agnes, daughter of the King of Bohemia, and she, inebriated also with the same wine, has refused the imperial dignity almost as though it were a poisonous reptile, and grasping the triumphal banner of the Cross goes forward to meet the Bridegroom accompanied by a choir of virgins. This indeed is the work of Almighty God, a new work accomplished on earth when Saint Elizabeth opened her heart to Jesus Christ conceived Him by love, brought Him again to birth in the world by charity, fed Him and cared for Him.

Our enemy the devil raises up two high walls to hide the eternal light from our eyes, namely spiritual ignorance blinding man to the power of God, and the love of our Redeemer, and the concupiscence of the body; but Saint Elizabeth safely ensconced in the shelter of humility overthrew both these walls, and having put the clouds of pride to flight she could enjoy the inaccessible and divine light. She cut at the very root of concupiscence, bridling all her affections in order to come to the true Love.

Vas admirabile; this vase is made of the gold of pity, the precious stones of wisdom ornamented with imperishable works into which the Lord has poured so many proofs of divine grace that through this vase which is Elizabeth earthly anger and envy, in themselves worthy of eternal death, might be purified. Thus God has shown what riches, what abundance of grace were contained in her whom the Lord prepared for eternal glory.

God created her in His image to make her share in His beatitude. She kept the thought of Him always in her heart, and kept the lamp of charity ever burning with works and this charity was not to be extinguished by floods or winds, nor by the thorns of tribulation and anguish.

Indeed the Virgin Mother of God has already brought her into the heavenly chamber of the Bridegroom, who has set a crown of ineffable glory on her head. While the Church Triumphant rejoices in her presence, the Church Militant is enriched by many miracles through the merits of this blessed one.

Beloved daughter, We have had two motives in setting before thee the example of Saint Elizabeth as a most precious pearl; first that thou mays't often look into the mirror of her example and consider if anything in thy own conscience offends the divine Majesty so that nothing may be lacking to thee of what is needful in a bride of Jesus Christ, and that so when thou art called to appear before the eternal King He may see thee too ornamented with every virtue and precious work.

The Pope does not explicitly mention Elizabeth's influence on Agnes, but obviously each cousin knew what the other was doing and to Agnes especially Elizabeth's achievement in Marburg, her whole life, her death would have been a vital inspiration. After having refused to consider marriage with Frederick or anyone else Agnes had given herself up to good works in Prague, where she too founded a hospital also dedicated to Saint Francis. Like Elizabeth, she worked in it herself "as any charwoman or cook, not with an angry or sour countenance, but with joy, and by her sweet face showing that she was a true servant of Jesus Christ." The family likeness is strong. On the death of King Otokar in 1229 her half-brother Wenceslaus came to the throne and he established the Franciscans in his capital and with his sister founded a convent of Poor Clares of which Agnes became abbess. She was guided by Saint Clare herself in four precious and revealing letters, and was also beatified.

The canonization of Saint Elizabeth was officially announced in Germany at Erfurt and the Archbishop of Mainz fixed that the translation of her body should take place in May, 1236. The foundation stone of the new church in Marburg to be dedicated to her was laid in May of 1235 and the work was carried on with incredible speed, so that the church was ready at the appointed time. The archbishops of Cologne, Trèves, and Mainz with all the bishops of Germany gathered in Marburg for the ceremony, and with them a host of abbots, prelates, princes, and people, for by now Elizabeth was claimed and acclaimed by rich and poor alike. Foremost among those present were her mother-in-law, the Landgräfin Sophie, the Landgraf Heinrich Raspe with his wife, Gertrude, Brother Conrad, who would soon be Grand Master of the Teutonic Order, and Elizabeth's three children, Hermann, now a big boy of fourteen, Sophie, only a little younger, and nine-year-old Gertrude, who had been brought from Altenberg. Surely Walther of Vargila, Isentrude, Guda, and the retainers from the Wartburg were there; and the faithful friends who had always believed in her must have felt their own degree heightened. All eyes were fixed on the Emperor, who appeared dressed as a penitent and barefoot but wearing a crown; he had asked for the honor of being among those to carry the body. Perhaps his gesture was partly political, and yet because Frederick was himself extreme in every direction his genius made him understand and appreciate the sanctity of Francis and Elizabeth. When the body was uncovered it was seen to be perfectly preserved, exhaling a very sweet scent, and from it came a fragrant oil. Frederick placed his own crown on Elizabeth's head and his words were reported: "Since I could not crown her as Empress in this world, I will at least crown her today, immortal queen in the kingdom of God." His letter to Brother Elias, Minister General of the Franciscan Order, repeats this devotion.

Twenty years had not yet passed since the girl Elizabeth had disturbed her family and the congregation in Eisenach by taking off her crown and laying it at the feet of the Crucifix. Did the Landgräfin Sophie recall the incident?

Macabre details of the subsequent treatment of Saint Elizabeth's body to satisfy the insatiability of relic hunters make us realize how wise Brother Elias had been in arranging the translation of Saint Francis' body as he did. He insured that it should remain intact.

The Knights of the Teutonic Order continued in charge of the beautiful Gothic church which was soon enriched with a fine rood screen and glass windows depicting scenes from Elizabeth's life; the inscription on the glass emphasizes her connection with the Third Order: *"Institutio Ordinis Tertiarorum."* Precious above all is the casket reliquary made to contain her body which was commissioned by her daughter Sophie, who surely had a voice in choosing the design and the scenes represented. For another three hundred years endless processions of pilgrims, rich and poor, sick and healthy came from all over Europe to pay homage to Elizabeth and to seek her help; the stones became worn with the knees of believers. Elizabeth, it seems, had wished for a steeple so high that the sound of the bell might reach Hungary; her name carried farther than any bell and brought many Hungarians to Marburg. Magnificent ceremonies and processions were frequent; Marburg became accustomed to the sight of emperors, kings, and colorful crowds, and though the great days of the Teutonic Order passed with the fourteenth century, the fame and glory of Saint Elizabeth's shrine continued as one of Christendom's holy places. Then came desecration. The Landgraf, Philip of Hesse, a descendant of the saint through her daughter, Sophie of Brabant, was a friend and follower of Luther. In 1539 despite energetic protests, in the presence of the Duke of Brunswick, the Count of Isenburg, and a large gathering, he insisted on opening the casket and gave orders that the bones should be thrown into the common grave. This, however, was not done, some bones were even restored to the sanctuary, others were dispersed, and a number of places claim to possess relics. The church in Marburg passed into Protestant hands. Many precious objects were lost, including Frederick's crown.

Let us turn back to the thirteenth century and catch sight of Elizabeth's children. Hermann had been at least partially brought up at the Wartburg, and we see him too for a moment through Joinville's eyes when he was at the court of France, and Queen Blanche of Castille used to kiss his forehead "with great devotion having heard that his mother had often kissed him thus." Both Saint Louis and his sister, Blessed Isabelle of France, followed the same path as Saint Elizabeth and shared her spirit. They were as tireless as she was in the service of God and others.

Having come of age at twelve, Hermann was associated with his uncle Heinrich Raspe in the government of Thuringia, and was engaged to a granddaughter of Frederick II. The engagement however was broken off when the quarrel between the Pope and the Emperor again flared up; in 1239 Hermann married Helen, daughter of Duke Otho of Brunswick, perhaps encouraged by his uncle who had also deserted the Hohenstauffen cause. Hermann died childless in 1241 and was buried beside his father in the abbey of Reinhardsbrunn.

Sophie married Duke Henri of Brabant as his second wife about 1239. The families were already connected, Heinrich Raspe having married for the third time Beatrice, a daughter of Duke Henri. The German princes were going through another period of terror before the threat of a renewed Mongol invasion, and Heinrich Raspe had ordered a crusade against the Asiatics to be preached by the Franciscans and Dominicans.

The danger passed, and Frederick II tried to regain Heinrich Raspe's allegiance; then, in 1242 Gregory IX died and his successor Innocent IV deposed the Emperor at the Council of Lyons in 1245. Heinrich Raspe continued to oppose Frederick's son Conrad, but already an ill man he fell from his horse and died childless in 1247. Thus ended the direct male line of the Thuringian dynasty and the Duchess Sophie claimed the Thuringian inheritance for herself and her children, the other claimants being her cousins Heinrich of Misnia and Hermann of Henneberg.

Sophie showed herself a true granddaughter of Hermann I, and for years carried on the dispute first against her cousins, and then with them against the Archbishop of Mainz. She married her own daughter Elizabeth to the Duke of Brunswick, and after endless skirmishes which entailed the division of Thuringia from Hesse, her son succeeded to the Hesse domains and through him and his sister Saint Elizabeth's descendants were multiplied in the great families of Germany and indeed of all Europe. Sophie, who died in 1284, was exceedingly pious and generous especially to those religious houses which were most active in promoting the cult of her mother.

Among these Altenberg was prominent, and after being brought up there Elizabeth's second daughter Gertrude became abbess of the community. Many of the nuns remembered Elizabeth's visits to the monastery, and her spinning of their wool; she had left an indelible impression kept alive by her daughter. Gertrude had inherited something of her mother's lovableness, and also her spirit of penance; she is recorded as saying: "the higher and more noble thou art the more thou must humble thyself in all things." It might be Elizabeth speaking; Gertrude probably learned those words sitting on her mother's lap. Sophie was accustomed to visiting her sister and through her Gertrude certainly heard of the great development in the Low Countries of the Feast of Corpus Christi. It was instituted in Liége in 1246 largely as the outcome of the vision of another Premonstratensian nun, Saint Juliana of Liége, and Gertrude introduced it at Altenberg in 1270 only four years before Saint Thomas Aquinas enriched the Church with the whole Office of Corpus Christi. From then onward Christians sang the wonderful *Lauda Sion Salvatorem*, the *Pange Lingua,* and the *Adoro Te.* Francis and Clare did not know these songs or the glory of the feast, but in Italy they were protagonists of devotion to the Blessed Sacrament, teaching which Elizabeth knew through the Franciscans in Germany.

Altenberg was not a rich monastery but Gertrude built the Gothic church which is reminiscent of the one in Marburg; she also built a hospital adjoining the monastery and like her mother worked in it herself. She died in 1297 in the odor of sanctity and was beatified.

We cannot help wishing that the two sisters had left some personal record of their mother. All through their lives they must have kept the impress of those early years when Elizabeth was their wonderful, and perhaps often bewildering, young mother who would appear at one moment dressed as a princess, and at another almost as a beggar. Sophie and Hermann could remember their father, and their mother's grief at the news of his death. Above all, they remembered her as always giving, and teaching them to deny themselves and give for love of Christ, and never to refuse the appeal of any suffering human being who might cross their path. How tender she always was with them; they remembered the touch of her hand, her smile, her laugh, her arms thrown round them always there to console them with a kiss, and no one talked of Jesus as she did. Then came the separation which had seemed so mysterious, culminating in that day in Marburg when, standing there with their grandmother and uncles and all the family, they had seen her for the last time with the Emperor setting a crown on her head and the whole world acclaiming her. They must have answered many questions carried away by time with the answers:

with pride they habitually signed themselves "son (or daughter) of Saint Elizabeth."

There is a tradition of a third daughter also named Sophie who became a Benedictine abbess, which would bring Elizabeth's children to four, but there is no proof of her existence and surely it would not have passed unrecorded.

And what of Guda and Isentrude, the friends Elizabeth so loved? The only trace of the latter is in the title given her in the deposition she made before the commissioners for Elizabeth's canonization, where she is called *"Ysentrudis, religiosa de Hursilgowe."* The traces of Guda are also vague, but it seems possible to identify her with a *"Jutta religiosa"* who made a vow at Elizabeth's tomb in 1232. In a sermon which formerly was attributed to Saint Bonaventure, Guda is spoken of as eating neither meat nor fish and drinking no wine, and Father Lemmens thinks that the sermon was written by Brother Conrad of Saxony who was Guda's confessor. According to the chronicle of Reinhardsbrunn Guda lived at Horselgau and was known as a singularly holy person with a gift of healing. When she died the monks of Reinhardsbrunn insisted on burying her in the abbey and miracles were recorded at her tomb.

In the Hungarian dynasty violence and sanctity continued to alternate; King Bela IV, Saint Elizabeth's brother, had two daughters — Saint Margaret, a Dominican nun who was remarkable for her spirit of humility, penance, and prayer, and Cunegonde, who married Duke Boleslaus of Poland and as a widow founded the Poor Clare monastery where she died; she too was beatified. Saint Elizabeth's great niece, the other Elizabeth who was born a princess of Aragon in 1271, had some of the same characteristics as her great aunt. For her, too, life consisted in complete self-donation; her spirit of penance and charity was supreme, so too her power of peacemaking, and even as a girl she was able to bring about peace in a family rent by wars and quarrels. She was devoted to her husband,

King Denis of Portugal, and to her children; as a widow she retired to the Poor Clare monastery of Coimbra where she died as a sister of the Third Order.

The French kinsfolk could boast of Saint Louis IX, his sister blessed Isabelle of France, and Saint Louis of Toulouse, and more remotely blessed Elzear and Delphine of Provence. King Louis IX seemed born to impersonate the just man described in Psalm 14; his passion for justice was equaled by his charity, and almost any day the King could be seen serving lepers, feeding the hungry, protecting the helpless, caring for the sick and poor, and when necessary as during the Crusade, burying the dead. In Joinville's pages King Louis is such a vivid figure that we seem to be standing before him. He once wrote to his daughter: "Dear daughter, let one desire to please God be always in your heart, and so dispose yourself that if you were certain never to be rewarded for any good you may do, or punished for any evil nevertheless you would keep yourself from anything displeasing to Him, and give your heart to all that might please Him, solely for love of Him." These words are his testament to the Franciscan Third Order of which he is the patron.

It is Mechtilde of Magdeburg who tells us that Saint Elizabeth was sent to convert the unhappy worldly people living in castles, and that many followed her example. There was something about Elizabeth that opened the eyes of others, and the blind who received physical sight at her tomb were only a few of those who through her saw new light, new joy, and new beauty. The example could hardly have been more dramatic; everyone could see the tremendous physical courage in facing voluntary self-discipline, poverty, cold, and every discomfort combined with the endless task of providing for the needs of the ill, cleaning, washing, staying up at night, always on her feet, regardless of fatigue, always smiling, always comforting and encouraging. Her moral courage was of the same caliber, and her story shows no instance of its ever having failed. Such an example opened people's eyes to misery and abuses they had somehow taken for granted, but which now appeared as urgently demanding a remedy. It challenged each individual; and habitual kindness and generosity looked very pale compared with Elizabeth's vision of Christ living in each of His suffering members. Our Lord Himself was within the reach of everyone, close at hand, waiting to be noticed, served, and loved. Not, however, only in the hospital, but in each circumstance of life, in every facet of her personality, Elizabeth showed them God. Now they realized that the scruples and self-abnegation which had once seemed tiresomely exaggerated were the signs of her incessant and immediate response to the divine call. Above all Elizabeth's joyful serenity in the midst of a sea of troubles perforce opened the eyes of the worldly and unhappy to completely new possibilities. Such joy is a proof that God's promises cannot fail, and that our Lord's lovers who share the cross with Him, even in this world share in His triumph, and heaven does begin on earth.

With a new understanding of Elizabeth many people wished to follow her in wearing the patched habit of the Franciscan Order of Penance, and soon she was acclaimed as the Patroness of Francis' Tertiaries living in the world. She and Saint Louis acted like magnets in attracting people of all kinds, many saints among them, many geniuses, and an innumerable number of those "ordinary" people who mattered so much to Francis, and who through his Third Order have been and are, at least occasionally, lifted out of the rut of selfishness into the clear air of supernatural faith and charity. Neither Francis nor his great followers have ever despised the seemingly small results; it is always worth taking a maximum of trouble to obtain even one incomplete good. Louis and Elizabeth are protagonists of the particular note of love inherent in the ideal of the Third Order; innumerable works of charity have borne, and bear Elizabeth's name; their history would fill volumes and they have passed through wars, revolutions, exile, persecution, and when cut down to the root in one place they spring up in another. Gregory

IX expressed the secret of this dynamic inspiration when he said: "By opening her heart to Jesus Elizabeth conceived Him by love, brought Him again to birth in the world by charity, fed Him and cared for Him."

In the Lower Church of Saint Francis in Assisi Simone Martini has painted Saint Clare and Saint Elizabeth standing side by side; it is one of the few instances where Elizabeth is shown dressed as a princess, and they are looking at each other. Did Simone realize how true an inspiration this was? Their human lives were very different, and yet they are inseparable; each in her own sphere followed the lonely path of sanctity with unflinching courage.

On the one hand, there is Clare who died at sixty after spending forty-two years of religious life in San Damiano in prayer, penance, poverty, and much physical suffering; her only desire was to be "hidden with Christ in God," united to Him through the cross. During those years of continuous heart to heart intimacy with our Lord Clare was not inactive, for the contemplative life is the highest and most fruitful of activities and nothing can be compared with it. The mistake is to separate contemplation and activity into arbitrary categories. Very often the contemplative who apparently leaves the world receives from God an added warmth of love for all men and an added sense of union with them. This is inevitable: the longer the sun's rays the greater the space between them; souls far from God are far from each other, and those who approach nearest to God in prayer are nearer to other souls many thousand miles away than perhaps we are to those with whom we live. Clare's conception of the contemplative life was an apostolic co-operation with God in the saving of souls; contemplative prayer opens a channel for the divine grace to flow into the world, and it may happen that any of us is able to overcome a temptation today because an unknown contemplative is praying and doing

WARTBURG CASTLE

A PASSAGE IN WARTBURG CASTLE

WARTBURG COURTYARD

(*Marburg Kunstinstitut*)

ENTRANCE TO WARTBURG CASTLE

ST. CLARE AND ST. ELIZABETH

Simone Martini. Assisi.

St. Elizabeth

Hans Holbein
Munich
(Marburg Kunstinstitut)

St. Elizabeth

Herman Rode
Reval
(Marburg Kunstinstitut)

penance at the other side of the globe. Activity is bound to be sterile unless it is rooted in contemplation.

Then we turn to Elizabeth, less than half Clare's age when she died, and whose mission lay in the midst of the world. Fundamentally, however, it was the same as Clare's, for she too was singled out by God and called to go to the utmost limit of love through her consecration to Christ crucified; she too was completely faithful to this vocation. Like Francis, Elizabeth "was always occupied with Jesus," that is always at prayer, for just as it is possible for exterior peace and silence to be frustrated by the inner din of distracting and harmful thoughts, so outward activity can be united to inner calm and recollection.

We have read Conrad of Marburg's emphatic assertion: "Before God I declare that I have seldom found a woman more given to contemplation"; even the beautiful outward signs of her prayer were identical with those of Clare.

In these days when so much stress is laid on exterior activity and performance perhaps Elizabeth's chief message is to recall her own Third Order and all who want to work for God in the world to the vital necessity of increasing union with God through penance and incessant prayer, and this is possible in all times, in all places, and in all circumstances. "Pray without ceasing," was Saint Paul's teaching. Only through prayer can evil be defeated because it alone opens a channel enabling the power and love of God to flow into our lives. Elizabeth's charity was the expression of her union with God; her superhuman practical accomplishment was the flowering of grace.

Clare and Elizabeth were equally in love with poverty and ready to fight for it. From the earliest times certain men and women have voluntarily cast off not only what is morally corrupt, but what is good and beautiful because they were and are irresistibly drawn by the magnet of God. Self-mastery is only part of the reason, and the poverty of the saints is not more negative than it is negative to deprive oneself of a precious object in order to give it to someone we love, or to offer that person our time and service and devotion. Above all, the gift is valuable because it is a gauge of love; giving is one of the chief luxuries of life. Do we dare to think we can give to God when everything we have is His gift? But God's gifts are free, given us to use as we choose, and He has told us over and over again that He does and will accept our gifts even to the cup of cold water, if they are a token of love. We see the costliness of sacrifice, but the saints know that to offer sacrifice is a magnificent priestly office, and that to give God the best, the dearest, the most beautiful things they possess is to be already on the threshold of heaven. Our Lord's example and teaching is the one never changing pattern of sanctity and His whole life was voluntary sacrifice and poverty. Francis, Clare, and Elizabeth with their eyes riveted on Jesus threw away their possessions, heedless of everything else because in the outpouring of their love they had to give God all they had and were, and felt that it was nothing. All other, lesser values disappeared but this poverty, this literal following of Christ did not leave them in a void but drew them closer to immense numbers of people and opened the way to astounding practical results. They loved poverty because our Lord had been born in a cave, had lived and worked in poverty, had not known where to lay His head, had died in poverty and been buried in another man's tomb. To be in a position of becoming voluntarily poor for love of Him was in itself privilege and riches, and through this renunciation they acquired new liberty, new power, unsuspected riches and their lives bear witness to the truth of the words of Jacopone da Todi, one of the greatest of Franciscan poets:

"Poverty is nothing having,
And yet all things possessing
In the spirit of liberty."

All sanctity is a sharing in the mystery of Christ, in His Passion, but also in His Resurrection, and the Church lays such stress on virginity because it is a foretaste of that Resurrection and of the life of heaven where a choir of virgins accompanies the Lamb wherever He goes; it is a direct participation in the beauty of God even during this life. The beauty of physical virginity as well as spiritual was Clare's, and yet she showed herself the true mother of her sisters in San Damiano. With what love they spoke of her when they were called as witnesses in the Cause of her canonization; they all emphasized her gentleness, her kindness, and the tenderness of her care for their bodies as well as their souls. Clare left her home and all earthly attachments, but today twelve thousand Poor Clares call her "our Mother." In a certain sense she was also the mother of Francis' vocation. He longed for the contemplative life, the "life of angels" as he called it; he consulted Clare whether the active apostolate were indeed God's will for him, or whether instead he might turn to pure contemplation in some hermitage far from the distraction of other men. After long prayer Clare told him that the active life was to be his; he submitted at once and gave a perfect example of contemplation expressed in activity.

Elizabeth too knew the attraction of virginity in the enclosed contemplative life which God had not willed for her, but in the midst of the world she kept that virginity of heart and soul which is dedicated to Him alone. Because of this she is a living witness to the light of Christ which is charity, a witness to the truth of Saint John's words that to those who receive Him, our Lord gives "the power to be made sons of God."

Unlike Clare, Elizabeth knew the full beauty and joy of being a human mother, and of having perfectly loved another human being. She might have devoted herself entirely to her three children, and that would have been something great and lovely, but also limited because God was asking more of her and giving her a special mission. Our blessed Lady became the mother of Jesus in unimaginable joy, but it needed the corresponding depth of anguish beneath the cross for her to become the mother of all of us. In the hard sacrifice of giving up the immediate care and pleasure of her children Elizabeth, too, took a far larger family into her arms to hold, to love, and to bring to God together with her own son and daughters. She did it first of all in the most direct and practical way possible; she has never ceased doing it since her death.

In all this she did not lose or give up her own children in any essential sense, for love embraces and unites all who are close to each other in God. Idolization and sentimentality can separate, but never love. Our blessed Lady did not lose her Son when she consented to be the mother of all living things; and so too on an infinitely lower level, which however is still divine, Elizabeth did not lose her children when she accepted the call of God to be a witness on earth to His charity and cherished and comforted the leper girl or the paralyzed boy in the place of Hermann and Sophie. She is a living example of the truth of Saint John's words: "We know that we have passed from death to life because we love the brethren." Elizabeth's whole short life was an ever increasing realization of love; like Francis, she was called to show how the love of God can transfigure, illuminate, and enhance all human love when it is grafted into the divine love. Each step of her way was a passing from what is perishable to what is eternally alive because it is rooted and founded in love; for her love was synonymous with life.

It is the unifying power of love that brings the saints so near to us. Our Lord tells us that He came to bring us new and more abundant life, and that "if anyone love Me and keep My words My Father will love him, and We will come and make Our abode with him." In Holy Communion God comes into every baptized soul in a state of grace, and the Blessed Trinity lives in that soul. Where God is, there is the Church Triumphant, the Church of Purgatory, the Church Militant, and Our Lord's prayer begins to be fulfilled that "all may be one." There is then no distance between the saints and such souls, who already share in the new song of love, the song of Christ's

victory over death, darkness and sin; only the truth is so wonderful that we are blinded by its light.

We see seven centuries of history between Francis, Clare,
Elizabeth, and ourselves, but that is only the drop scene and
of small importance in comparison with what lies behind. The
key to their union with God, to our union with them, to the
new and more abundant, more efficacious life of grace which
God wills to give us is love, and Elizabeth tells each of us that
the innermost secret of life is "God is my only love."

Both Clare and Elizabeth are donors. No one ever approached
them during their earthly lives who did not go away enriched,
materially as far as was in their power, spiritually to an unlimited
degree. They gave up everything, but God filled their hands,
and far beyond the food and clothing they gave was the comfort,
the joy that God chose to communicate to others through
them. In the spiritual life nothing can remain stagnant and
thus having nothing Clare and Elizabeth possessed all things
and became two channels of life-giving grace. Their mission of
giving began in this world and after their death it increased in
the measure that heaven transcends earth; they are giving to
us all the time. While they were alive even they had sometimes to refuse at least the material gift; now there is no refusal
possible, and their giving will always surpass our asking.

We go out into the world and see seven centuries of history
between Francis, Clare, Elizabeth, and ourselves and we ask
are these lives really relevant to our uncertain and confused
world which questions every positive assertion as to the meaning of life not made in the name of "science," and on the social
plane is absorbed in standards of living and organized welfare
and to a great extent absorbed in having the best time
obtainable.

How does this choice of poverty and penance affect us?
Essentially it has exactly the same significance today as in the
thirteenth century. All our technical achievements have not
lessened our pride and selfishness and our Lord's perfectly clear

words to take up the cross and follow Him which inspired Francis, Clare, and Elizabeth continue to inspire a minority, and to challenge all of us who accept the Christian faith. Our hospitals are not those of Elizabeth's day, but with all our organization she would still find plenty to do were she physically among us; there is always place for individual charity.

The intervening history between her and us is of small importance in comparison with what lies behind — the finding of love as the innermost secret of life, which once found is timeless. Elizabeth found it and gives us the key to her own and all the saints' union with God and to our union with them, the key to the more abundant and efficacious life of grace which God wills to give us in an unending stream renewing our spiritual life at each moment. "God is my only love." Elizabeth's whole life is in those five words, and she still shows us how to put them into practice.

APPENDIX

DEPOSITION MADE BEFORE THE COMMISSIONERS FOR THE CAUSE OF CANONIZATION

Guda's Relation

GUDA, a pious virgin who, when about five years old, had been given to blessed Elizabeth as companion, the latter being then about four years of age. When asked as to her life and conversation, Guda declared under oath that the same blessed Elizabeth, formerly Landgräfin of Thuringia and daughter of the King of Hungary, was given to the study and practice of religion from her childhood, directing all her will and activity toward God, both when occupied with serious matters, and when at play. While she was still ignorant of letters at about five years old, she frequently knelt down before the altar and opened the Psalter as though she were praying from it, and she gave prophetic signs of her good disposition in many secret genuflections, and cautiously seized any opportunity for entering the chapel. If she thought that any of the servant maids were watching she would play at catching the other little girls and being caught, and thus run toward the chapel, she would jump over the threshold and kneel down with hands joined and pray and prostrate herself before the altar. In the same way she used a hopping game as a means to approach the chapel in order at least to be able to kiss the threshold and walls. In a game played with rings she placed all her hope of winning in God, promising that should she win she would make a certain number of genuflections and *Aves*. If it proved impossible to fulfill this promise, she would suggest to the other little girls: "Let us all lie down side by side and measure who is the tallest," and this enabled her to make repeated genuflections as she herself later acknowledged. In the ring and other games she gave a tenth part of her earnings to girls poorer than herself with whom she played, and to whom she also made small presents, making them each promise to say a *Pater* and *Ave*.

While still young she had a particular devotion to Saint John the Evangelist as the guardian of purity. It was the custom of the court to draw lots among the Apostles for a protector, and this was done by inscribing each Apostle's name on candles or on bits of papers which were then heaped on the altar. Her prayer was answered when three times she drew the name of Saint John, and in his honor she never refused anything asked of her in his name, no matter whether it were the pardon of an offense or a favor.

When she was obliged to go to bed with her prayers incompleted she would continue them in bed; every day and in all things she studied to go against her own will for love of God. If she were winning a game, she would break it off saying: "That is enough success; I want to stop for love of God." So too when dancing she would say: "One turn is enough, let me give up the others too for love of God." She wished to be poor, and to offer God many small mortifications and she would not put on gloves or button on her sleeves before midday on Sundays. In these and other ways too she denied her body any indulgence and kept herself from the vanities of the world out of reverence for God; while still so young she had God always before her eyes, lovingly invoked Him in all things, and directed all her life toward Him. While still young she secretly endured oppression and many burdens in the castle of the family in which she was brought up. Harsh words and deeds, injustice and insults were inflicted on her by those who were filled with envy at the sight of the precocious goodness of her nature, and how her qualities increased with her bodily growth. But she bore everything with patience, placing her hope in God.

When of marriageable age she suffered grave and open persecution by those nearest to her, and at the hands of vassals who advised her future husband to repudiate her and send her home to the King her father. They asserted that her dowry was insufficient to such a family as that of her future husband, who, they declared, could make a far more profitable union among his powerful neighbors; and to this they tried to persuade him. Faced with this contempt, Elizabeth as usual put her whole trust in God, placing herself in His divine will, and against the advice and hope of others her bridegroom consoled her secretly in all her trouble and sadness. Guda added that much more could be said on this subject which she did not remember but this little was sufficient.

When asked how long she had been with blessed Elizabeth and how she knew all this, she repeated what has already been said, and also told how she had remained with blessed Elizabeth, and served her after the death of her husband the Landgraf until she had received the gray habit at the hands of Master Conrad. And Guda too put on the gray habit and confirmed the vow of chastity she made before Master Conrad several years earlier.

Isentrude, a religious of Hursilgowe was in the household of blessed Elizabeth for about five years during the lifetime of the Landgraf her husband, and after his death she remained there for more than a year as a familiar friend who knew all Elizabeth's secrets until she had put on the gray habit. When asked about the life of blessed Elizabeth, Isentrude affirmed on oath that during her husband's life Elizabeth was always very religious, humble, most charitable, and intent on many prayers. She, Isentrude, often followed Elizabeth, howbeit grumbling, when she hurried into the church and quickly made furtive genuflections. Elizabeth was still living in the pomp of the world, but secretly she took in ill beggars of dreadful aspect suffering from sores in their heads, and she cut off their hair and dressed their dreadful wounds, with her own hands tenderly embracing them. She did this in a space under the castle wall and there she secretly washed and anointed them, always avoiding being seen, and when the serving maids discovered her they would laugh.

Isentrude then said that blessed Elizabeth, with the consent of her husband, made a vow of obedience to Master Conrad in everything except what concerned her husband's rights. She promised to observe perpetual continence, and should she outlive her husband she would live in chastity, and she made this vow in the monastery of Saint Catherine in Eisenach. She then said that after blessed Elizabeth had made the vow of obedience to Master Conrad he admonished her that she must not make use of her husband's goods unless she was sure that they were honestly come by. This she strictly observed so that even as she sat beside her husband at table she abstained from all food obtained through extortion, and she never touched anything that she did not know to be lawfully obtained. Thus when she was being served she often pretended to eat the bread and other items of food by crumbling them and otherwise disposing of them.

With three companions who were in agreement with her, blessed Elizabeth begged the Landgraf not to be indignant if she behaved differently from the other persons at table; whereupon he answered: "Let her do as she will. If I did not fear the reproaches of those about me, I would hasten to offer more of my substance to God and do the same; please God I shall soon dispose differently of what concerns me."

With the money assigned to her, as a jointure blessed Elizabeth provided for her own needs and those of her maids, and when they were in a place where nothing could be bought she would send messengers to beg provisions from neighboring houses as though she preferred their food to that served in the court; she did this hoping thus to respect Master Conrad's order. He, however, forbade her to touch food from any source whose origin might offend her conscience. Thus it often happened that she suffered real hunger with a few small honey cakes as her only food. Of all the dishes served at the court table she would content herself with a little bread when this was legitimate, but her husband, distressed at seeing her hunger, would secretly warn her of what she might eat with a good conscience. At table she abstained from all the numerous delicacies, so much so that once five small birds were brought her of which she kept one for herself and sent the others to her followers, and this constituted her dinner. She suffered far more from her maids' deprivations than from her own when she could not conscientiously give them all they needed. Very often she inquired from the servants what food was legitimate, and then she would say: "Today we can eat," or again as regarding her husband's wine: "Today we can drink." And when she knew that everything was legitimate she would clap her hands in delight exclaiming: "Today we can both eat and drink."

It happened that she was on a journey with her husband who had to attend an important Diet, and there being no food that she could touch without offending her conscience she contented herself with coarse and stale black bread which she soaked in water and this was her whole dinner, for she was accustomed to fast every Saturday. She did this although on that day they rode eight German miles which are the equal of forty Italian miles. She kept up this singular and unusual way of living even though she suffered much obloquy on the subject, as did her husband for allowing it, but she bore it all with patience. She touched nothing obtained from illicit means, but as far as she could she did all in her power to provide for those who through her suffered deprivation.

Blessed Elizabeth often enjoined on her attendants that they should wake her at night in order to pray, and she was in the habit of rising every night when her husband slept, or seemed to sleep. Her attendants, fearing to disturb their lord and master, asked how she wished to be roused, and she told them to pull her foot. And it happened that the said Isentrude meaning to wake Elizabeth pulled the Landgraf's foot by mistake, he having crossed his leg with that of his wife. When it was explained to him what had happened unintentionally, he bore it with patience. Blessed Elizabeth often so prolonged her prayers that she would fall asleep on the carpet. When her attendants asked her why she did not get back into bed, she answered: "Even though I cannot always pray, I can always mortify my flesh by depriving it of the pleasure of being beside my beloved husband." She also rose secretly from her bed and made her attendants flagellate her, then, after she had prayed she got back gladly into her husband's bed; and this she did often after she had made a vow of obedience to Master Conrad, especially in Lent and on Fridays.

When her husband was absent blessed Elizabeth would pass whole nights in vigils, genuflections, scourgings, and prayer; she also put off her rich clothes and ornaments and dressed herself as a widow with a nun's veil on her head. She would wear harsh wool or haircloth next to her skin, even when she was outwardly dressed in magnificent apparel. When her husband was about to return, she adorned herself sumptuously, not she said, to gratify the body's pride, but for the honor of God, and in order to prevent any temptation to sin in her husband should he be displeased with her appearance. "It is in God," she said, "that I love my husband, and may He who sanctified marriage grant us eternal life."

When other ladies came to visit her, she spoke to them of God, urgently persuading them to a vow of abstinence and to avoiding all worldly vanities; if they could not give up the world entirely, at least she asked that they should restrain themselves in dancing and reduce the magnificence of their sleeves, which should be modest and decent, and they might give up the excessive adornment of their heads and the elaborate dressing of their hair. She would also plead with them that they should make a vow of continence in the event of their husband's death.

From her childhood blessed Elizabeth was in the habit of wearing neither sleeves nor rings or any other bodily ornament during the time of the Gospel and the Canon of the Mass and she appeared in the most humble posture especially when the priest held the Host in his hands. For her own purification after the birth of each of her children when other women went to church most richly adorned, blessed Elizabeth came to the church dressed in plain wool, barefoot, and carrying her child in her arms whom she then offered to the Blessed Virgin on her altar together with a candle and lamb. And after the ceremony after returning home she would give the dress and cloak she had worn to some poor woman. Again dressed in a plain woolen gown and barefoot she used to follow the Rogation procession and during the Station sermons she would take her place among the poorest of the women.

During her husband's lifetime she and her attendants spun the wool and then from the cloth prepared the habits of the Friars Minor and also clothes for the poor. They prepared clothes for catechumens and blessed Elizabeth would clothe them with her own hands, taking children to be baptized and holding them at the sacred font, and acting as godmother she became their benefactress.

She would also help to lay out the dead, clothe them and accompany them to the tomb; she once cut up a very large linen sheet in order that it should serve to wrap round several dead persons. If the poor and sick whom she visited were in debt and could not pay their creditors, blessed Elizabeth paid their debts. She would not allow the dead to be clothed in new linen or new shirts, but rather in old ones, saying that new shirts should be given to the poor. She frequently visited the poor in their own houses to console them, and when messengers arrived begging her help for other sick, she would inquire where they lived and would go to inspect their homes; roused to compassion and pity, no matter how great the distance or how bad and muddy the road she would seek them out in hovels, taking no account of filth, and there she would do whatever was necessary for them, consoling them with her gifts, her work, and her compassion. One day she wished to milk a cow to satisfy the desire of a poor person for some milk, but the cow was restive and would not allow it.

Master Conrad, whom she obeyed even during her husband's life, summoned her one day to a sermon, but she did not go owing to the arrival of the Marchioness of Misnia (probably her sister-in-law, Jutta). Master Conrad in anger sent to tell her that owing to her disobedience he would have no more to do with her. She hurried to see him the next day and humbly begged his forgiveness; despite this she and her attendants, clothed only in their undershirts, lay prostrate before him while he imposed their penance with many hard blows.

In that time there was a general famine, but Elizabeth trusted to Divine Providence to provide what was necessary for each day. The Landgraf had left home to attend the Diet in Cremona, and blessed Elizabeth caused the reserves of corn in his granaries to be expended to satisfy the needs of the poor, each day as much as was necessary. Beneath the high castle of the Wartburg there was a large building which she filled with a number of sick people for whom the general almsgiving could not suffice;

and despite the long steep hill she visited them several times a day, consoling them and encouraging them to patience, and she sold her own jewels in order to satisfy their needs. She paid no heed to the fetid air and to the stench of corruption made worse by the summer heat and which her attendants only bore with much murmuring; she, on the other hand, bore everything gaily and with her own hands treated the sick, cleaning their heads and faces, their mouths and spittle, their noses and ears.

At one time there were in this building a number of poor children for whom she provided everything and with much gentleness and kindness kept them near her, and as many as came in all ran to her calling her "mother." She paid the most loving care to the worst cases among these children, the deformed, the dirtiest, the weakest, those suffering from the most repulsive illnesses, and would take them tenderly into her arms. In order to keep these children amused she would send and buy glass rings and other playthings; once when she was carrying these things in her cloak they fell over a rock on to stones below but nothing was broken and they were all distributed to amuse the children.

These sick people shared in the general almsgiving, but beside this blessed Elizabeth chose the poorest and weakest and lodged them in a dwelling outside the castle where she fed them from her own table with her own hands, denying herself and her attendants many things in order to give them to the poor. One day after the usual distribution there was only a little beer left and this she gave to all present, and yet there remained as much in the jug as there had been before. When everyone was satisfied she would give shirts and shoes to all who could work, shoes, in order that their feet should not be hurt by the stubble, and she gave them sickles so that they should be able to work and thus support themselves.

To others who were too weak to work she gave clothes which they could sell in the market; she gave everything most gladly with her own hands, and even when she had given to all she still found single persons to whom she also gave something. If she had no money she gave the poor women cloaks, dresses, and other garments made of silk with the warning: "Do not use these things to satisfy your own vanity, but rather sell them and buy what is necessary and work hard." Among the women to receive such presents there was one who had been given shoes, a shirt, and an overdress at which she was so overjoyed that she fell to the ground and it seemed as though she would die, but then she cried out that never had she known such joy. Seeing her agitation Elizabeth became anxious lest her gifts might cause the woman's death.

While blessed Elizabeth was still living amidst the honors of her worldly rank her heart was already inclined to poverty, and she often spoke of it with her maids. In their presence in her own palace she would put on an old cloak, and cover her head with an old linen cloth saying: "This is how I shall look when I go begging and suffer misery and need for the love of God."

On Maundy Thursday she made a solemn distribution to the poor; on one particular Holy Thursday she summoned many lepers, washed their hands and feet herself, and humbly kneeling before them she kissed their wounds and terrible sores. When and wherever she found lepers she would sit down at their side and comfort them and encourage them to patience; she had as little fear of these sufferers as of a healthy person, and gave them copious alms.

She avoided all superfluous clothes and long and richly embroidered gowns. She performed all works of charity with cheerful friendliness, and had received the grace of shedding many tears in secret, but they flowed lightly down her face without ever distorting it. These and many other wonderful things she accomplished which are now passed for they were done during the lifetime of her husband with whom she lived in holy matrimony for they wonderfully loved each other, and each gently comforted and encouraged the other in the love and service of God. Because of his position the Landgraf was necessarily occupied with many earthly concerns, but inwardly he always kept the fear of God before his eyes and allowed the utmost freedom to blessed Elizabeth in all that she did to the honor of God and the welfare of her own soul.

In all this Guda and Isentrude being both under oath were in complete agreement, since they lived together with Elizabeth as part of the household.

After the death of her husband blessed Elizabeth, however, was driven from the castle and from the property which belonged to her jointure by some of her husband's vassals. Her husband's brother was then still young. She went down into the city that lies at the foot of the castle hill, and lodged in a poor dwelling adjoining a tavern, which had formerly been used as a pig sty, and where some of the innkeepers' belongings were stored. She spent that night in great gladness; about midnight she went to the church of the Friars Minor and begged them to sing the *Te Deum* of Matins as a song of her praise and joy for her tribulations. During the next day none of the rich citizens of the place dared to take her in, and she and her maids entered a church and sat there a long time. When the children were brought down to her from the castle she did not know where to turn to find a shelter for them against the icy cold of winter, even though the children as heirs of their father were masters of the place. Driven by need she went at last to the house of a priest begging him to have pity on her and the children. Afterward she was brought into the house the proprietor of which was opposed to her; a small room was placed at her disposal into which she and her family were crammed although there were other unoccupied rooms in the house. She left the house after being insulted by her host and his wife, and took leave of the walls that had protected her from rain and cold with the words: "I would gladly thank the human beings but I should not know for what." Finding no other shelter, she returned to her first dirty lodging by the inn.

Persecuted by her husband's vassals for no reason, and deprived of her own property she suffered much hardship and sent her children to various places where they could be brought up. Even then she saved some of her own scanty food to give to the poor.

An old sick woman who had often been helped with alms and care in her infirmity met blessed Elizabeth on the way to church along a narrow path and where some steppingstones had been placed in order to facilitate the crossing of a deep muddy pool. The old woman would not give way and pushed blessed Elizabeth over so that she fell into the muddy water, and all her clothes were draggled and wet. This too she bore with patience and got up laughing and merrily washed her clothes.

One day during Lent she leaned kneeling against the wall and remained a long time with her eyes fixed on the altar. When at last she came to herself and took some food for she was very weak, she began to sweat and still leaning against the wall sank into the arms of the said Isentrude. Everyone except her two maids had to leave the room. She kept her eyes wide open looking out of the window, and started to laugh merrily; then after an hour she shut her eyes crying bitterly, then again she opened them smiling as before; thus she continued till Compline in contemplation alternating between eyes shut in grief and open-eyed in gladness, but the latter prevailed. After a long silence she suddenly exclaimed: "If Thou, O Lord, wilt remain with me, I will always be Thine, and never let anything separate me from Thee." The said Isentrude (a noble lady and more intimate with her than her other maids) asked her to tell them with whom she had spoken. At first Blessed Elizabeth was unwilling, but at last gave way before Isentrude's insistence: "I saw heaven open and my dear Lord Jesus bent down to me comforting me in my various troubles and anxieties, and when I saw Him I was overjoyed and laughed, but when He turned away His Face as though to leave me, then I cried. 'If thou wilt be with Me, I will be with thee.' Thereupon I answered Him as you heard."

Isentrude then begged her to describe the vision she had had in the church during the consecration of the Host, as has been recounted. Blessed Elizabeth answered: "What I then saw cannot be repeated, but believe me I was in the utmost joy and saw the marvelous secrets of God."

After this her aunt, the abbess of Kitzingen, who was her mother's sister, filled with pity for the sufferings and plight of blessed Elizabeth summoned her and also caused her to meet with her uncle the Lord Bishop of Bamberg. He showed her all honor, but wished her to remarry which he also told her. This caused great distress to blessed Elizabeth's above-mentioned maids who had made a vow of chastity together with her, but she comforted them saying repeatedly: "I have complete trust in God; He knows that when I made the vow of chastity during my husband's lifetime I did it in all purity and sincerity of heart, and trusting in His mercy I hold it to be impossible that He should fail to protect my chastity against all human attack and human power, all the more because I made that vow unconditionally with no stipulation that it should please my friends or that God should show me something else. I made an absolute unconditional vow to observe chastity should my husband die. If my uncle insisted on my marrying against my will, I would defend myself in every way, even to cutting off my nose, so that no man would even look at such a mutilated fright."

Against her will she was taken to the castle of Pottenstein to wait there until arrangements for her remarriage were completed; she understood all this and placed all her hope and trust in God that He would preserve her chastity. And He who is the comforter of the afflicted did not fail, for suddenly there arrived a messenger from the Bishop that she was to return immediately to Bamberg to be present at the reception of her husband's bones which were being brought back from the distant land where he died.

The Bishop went with a stately procession to meet the Landgraf's body, and with many tears Elizabeth said: "Lord, I thank Thee that in Thy pity Thou has given me the comfort of seeing the longed for bones of my husband. Thou knowest that though I loved him so dearly I do not regret that my beloved obeyed Thy will which was also my will, and sacrificed himself for the Holy Places. I would give the whole world if I might have him back, and would willingly go begging with him. I call Thee, however, to witness that against Thy will I would not call him back to this life even if I could do so at the price of one single hair. I commend him and myself to Thy mercy, may Thy holy will be accomplished in us."

After the burial of her husband's bones in the abbey of Reinhardsbrunn blessed Elizabeth returned to Thuringia with those of her husband's vassals who had brought home his body. Her uncle the Bishop would not have entrusted her to these nobles had they not promised to protect her interests and to obtain for her the free use of her jointure.

Blessed Elizabeth, however, continued to live in poverty and want until at the command of Master Conrad she went to Marburg. There she put on the gray habit of the poor Sisters which was poor and old, and at different times she distributed about two thousand marks to the poor, this being the money she received as compensation for her jointure. On one day she gave away five hundred marks to the crowd of the needy who had come to beg for help. She also gave away all that remained of the jewels she had brought with her from her Father the King of Hungary, and founded a hospital in Marburg. She endured many insults and much contumely from the nobles and the people of that place; the nobles declared her to be mad and forbade their dependents to have anything to do with her, and said many harsh things about her. She bore all this with much joyful patience, for which they reproached her saying that she had forgotten her husband's death very quickly, and instead of being joyful she should be mourning. Because Master Conrad had insisted that she should despise all earthly things she prayed earnestly that God should detach her from everything of this world, that she should overcome even the love for her children, and not heed the insults and criticism of others. After she prayed thus she said to her maids: "God has heard my prayer; I despise all the worldly goods I once cared for; and God be my witness I now love my children with the same love as I have for all my fellow creatures. I have given these children to God, to do with them as He wills. I gladly accept calumny, contempt, and insults, my only love is God."

In many ways Master Conrad tested her endurance, breaking her will and giving her orders that were against all her inclination. In order to try her he sent away one by one the maids she loved so that she was hurt by each single parting. At last he drove away me, Isentrude, whom she loved above all, and with much grief and many tears she saw me depart. Finally he sent away my companion Guda who had been with her since they were children and whom she loved most especially; and blessed Elizabeth parted from her too with tears and deep sorrow. Master Conrad of blessed memory did this in praiseworthy zeal and with the intention that she should no longer be able to speak with us of anything connected with her former grandeur and perhaps be tempted to regret it. Besides this he deprived her of all human comfort because he wished her to think only of God. Some stern women were assigned to her as companions and she suffered from their oppressions. They spied upon her cunningly according to Master Conrad's order, and reported to him any infringement of her vow of obedience, or when she gave away alms to the poor either directly or through a third person. Later Master Conrad himself controlled her donations, for she kept nothing of what she had and gave everything to the poor.

Through the accusations of her companions she often suffered hard blows from Master Conrad who also boxed her ears; these blows she had greatly desired in memory of those suffered by our Lord. Blessed Elizabeth was so obedient to Master Conrad that when we, Isentrude and Guda, went to see her she would not speak to us without his permission, nor could she give us any refreshment. All the contempt, the blows, and trials were heaped upon her by the praiseworthy zeal of Master Conrad in order that she should not falter in her resolution; and she bore everything with the greatest patience and fidelity.

The pious women Isentrude and Guda were unanimous in their report of blessed Elizabeth's life; they had lived in the intimacy of the Landgraf and Blessed Elizabeth and gave their testimony upon oath. When they were interrogated each singly how they had known all this, each answered that she had lived for many years with blessed Elizabeth. . . .

Elizabeth, a former servant of blessed Elizabeth the Landgräfin of Thuringia, upon oath declared that she had been for some time with blessed Elizabeth after her clothing in the gray habit of poverty, and she had seen her many works of charity and observed her deep humility. During the period when she lived in Marburg she took into her house many poor, weak, ill, and pious persons all of whom she served herself. She prepared the food with her servants who had also vowed themselves to God and taken the gray habit; she served the poor in the hospital, washing them, making their bed, and covering them. A one-eyed child covered with scurvy had been taken into the house and she often carried him to perform his natural wants and treated him with all imaginable kindness.

Irmingarde, a pious woman who had been clothed with the gray habit, declared upon oath that she had been maid to blessed Elizabeth and saw how, after her acceptance of the gray habit she took the poor of Marburg into her house, nursed and served them. Besides what she did in the hospital she gave away much to other poor, and would secretly sell golden rings, silken gowns, and other precious things in order to help the needy. Irmingarde also spoke of the one-eyed boy with scurvy whom blessed Elizabeth would carry six times in the night to satisfy his natural wants, after which she would put him back to bed, and cover him; she would wash the dirty clothes of this boy herself, and reassured him with many endearing words. Irmingarde also told how after the building of the Marburg hospital blessed Elizabeth helped to wash the sick and put them to bed, covering them warmly. Once she took a large fine linen cloth such as is used to adorn a house, and used it to bathe the poor, and to cover them and she did this with the words: "How happy we are to be able to wash and cover our Lord." To this one of her maids answered: "I do not know if we all feel like that."

She also told how blessed Elizabeth took in a leper girl of dreadful appearance, covered with wounds and sores, at whom no one could look even from afar. Blessed Elizabeth, however, nursed her in the hospital, treated her wounds with ointment, bound them up, knelt down to untie her shoe laces, and had the girl allowed it would also have taken off her shoes. She cut her finger- and toenails, tenderly stroking her disfigured face, and all were unanimous in saying that the girl permanently recovered her health. Blessed Elizabeth had placed this girl in an isolated room of the house, but often went to see how she was, calling the girl into her room, talking and laughing with her, and would make her bed. She was most gentle in her speech with the poor, and most zealous in giving them all that they wished for. She constantly admonished them not to neglect the baptism of their children; she would accompany others to confession in order that they should receive Holy Communion. Once having in vain urged a poor old woman to confess her sins she gave her a beating for the old woman lay there dead drunk and was too lazy to move. Since she would not listen to words she was finally driven to confession by blows.

After her husband's death blessed Elizabeth was deprived by her brother-in-law of the use of her jointure. She could have enjoyed her own maintenance at the table of her husband's brother, but she refused to be fed with what had been extorted from the poor, as happens in many princely houses, and pre-

ferred to be outcast and to earn her food by the work of her
own hands. As is well known she used to spin wool for the
monastery of Altenberg, and the price paid her was less than
it should have been. She also gave alms to the Church from
her earnings.

Irmingarde also told how blessed Elizabeth would even spin
when she was in bed, and ill; she did not know how to spin
flax. Even when she took the distaff from blessed Elizabeth's
hand wishing her to rest, she would continue to prepare the
wool for future work. During that time she caused some big
fish to be sold which had been sent her as a present. They were
sold by Brother Heinrich, son of the Graf von Wegebach, who
was first a hermit and later became a Friar Minor. She sent the
fish to be sold because she needed the money.

Now it happened that the King of Hungary, the father of
blessed Elizabeth, sent a Count named Pavias with a considerable following to accompany his daughter back to her native
land. This was because he had heard that she was living in
the utmost poverty, deprived of any comfort. When this Count
arrived in Marburg he found blessed Elizabeth spinning wool;
making the sign of the cross and greatly astonished he said:
"Never before has it been seen that a King's daughter should
be spinning." She loved poverty and banishment so deeply that
nothing would persuade her to return to Hungary with her
father's messenger. Her gray cloak was very short and blessed
Elizabeth lengthened it with a bit of stuff of another color; she
also patched her torn sleeves in the same way. Once in the
winter not having sufficient to cover herself she lay between
two coverlets; she would also lie on the ground saying: "I lie
here as in my coffin," and she merrily endured affliction.

Once when blessed Elizabeth had been summoned by her
aunt, the abbess of Kitzingen, she was ordered by her aunt to
have a bath. But she only splashed the water with her foot
calling out: "I have finished with the bath," and quickly left
the bathroom. On one occasion while blessed Elizabeth was

busy with the aforesaid work through which she earned her bread, she was summoned to Eisenach by Master Conrad. Having been paid in advance for her work she sent back a Cologne penny with the unspun wool to Altenberg for she would not keep more than she had actually earned.

Elizabeth, maid to blessed Elizabeth, also declared on oath that a noble lady, Gertrude von Leinbach, came to visit blessed Elizabeth bringing with her a lad named Berthold who was fashionably clothed. Blessed Elizabeth called him to her saying: "You appear arrogant; why do you not serve your Creator?" To which the youth answered: "O my Lady, I beg you to pray for me that God may give me the grace to serve Him." She again said: "Do you wish me to pray for you?" and he replied: "Yes, I do." Blessed Elizabeth then told him: "This being so you too must earnestly beg for God's grace in prayer and I will gladly pray with you." And according to her habit she at once threw herself on her knees in the cloister of the monastery in Wehrda where she was, and began to pray earnestly for the youth, who meanwhile had sought out another spot in the monastery in which to pray. After both had prayed for some time the youth called out in a loud voice: "O my Lady, stop praying!"

But blessed Elizabeth continued in ardent prayer. After another interval the youth called out still louder: "O my Lady, stop praying: I am fainting." He was so inflamed with heat that his whole body was in a sweat and steaming and as though beside himself he threw about his arms and whole body. Then the mother of the tormented youth and the said Elizabeth, maid to blessed Elizabeth still under oath, said that together with Irmingarde they hurried to the youth and found him as has been said so overheated that his clothing was wet with sweat and his voice rose ever higher as he called: "For God's sake stop praying, or I shall be consumed by this fire." Those who were holding him could hardly endure the heat to their hands; but as soon as blessed Elizabeth ended her prayer the youth felt better; immediately after blessed Elizabeth's death he entered the order of the Friars Minor. What has here been related happened to the youth a year before the death of blessed Elizabeth; many other similar things took place as told by the same maid Elizabeth.

After having endured extreme poverty blessed Elizabeth received a large sum as her jointure and she summoned the poor within a radius of twelve miles round Marburg for a certain day and gave orders that five hundred marks should be distributed among them. In order that everything should proceed in order blessed Elizabeth having put on an apron went among the people inviting them to sit down so that she might serve them according to the example of our Lord. It was announced that any person who left his or her place in an attempt to obtain twice of the alms thus setting a bad example and disturbing the others, should have a lock of hair cut off. It so happened that a girl named Hildegunde who had most beautiful hair had heard nothing of this injunction and was there not to receive any alms but to find her sick sister. However, she was taken to blessed Elizabeth as though she were guilty of disobeying the order, and the blessed one asked of what she was guilty and on seeing the girl's magnificent hair at once ordered it to be cut off. Upon this the girl began to cry bitterly, and several persons approached blessed Elizabeth and explained that the girl was entirely innocent and had been unjustly punished. Blessed Elizabeth answered: "At least now she will not go and dance with that magnificent hair." She recalled the girl and inquired whether she had never thought of serving God more perfectly, to which the girl replied that she had indeed long thought of serving God as a nun, but could not bring herself to part with her magnificent hair. Then blessed Elizabeth said: "I am more glad that you have lost this hair than I should have been had my son become emperor." And the girl was clothed in the gray habit and entered the hospital as a servant; her wonderful hair is still preserved in the Marburg hospital. Hildegunde told this under oath and it was confirmed by the parish priest, and many other persons with him.

In the evening after Blessed Elizabeth had given away the alms of five hundred marks, many poor and ill folk had remained lying on the steps of the hospital and in the courtyard for it was too late for them to start home, and already the moon had risen. They had been left behind by those who were stronger and had already left. When blessed Elizabeth saw this she said to her companions: "Look at these poor weak people; we must give them something." So to each were given six Cologne pennies and she insisted that the children should have the same sum as their elders. She also gave bread to all after which she said: "We must make these folk happy, let us light a fire for them." And so a fire was lighted and she saw to it that their feet were washed and rubbed with ointment, after which the people feeling refreshed began to sing. When Elizabeth heard it she said to those about her: "Didn't I tell you, one must make people happy," and she joined merrily in their gaiety.

Still under oath, the maid Elizabeth told how once when blessed Elizabeth was in Wehrda there was there a poor woman about to give birth to a child. Her own hospital being far away blessed Elizabeth prepared a barn next to her own dwelling, lighted the fire, and prepared a bed with cushions and blankets and all that was necessary for the woman. When the child was born blessed Elizabeth carried it to be baptized giving it her own name, blessed the mother, and cared for her entirely during the following month. At the end of this time she gave the woman a cloak, her own shoes, and other clothes together with twelve Cologne pennies; she also ordered her maid Elizabeth to cut the fur from her own sleeves so that the baby should be warmly wrapped up, and the woman also received bacon and flour and a pair of shoes for her husband. Unmindful of these benefits the poor woman took leave of blessed Elizabeth and went off with her husband, leaving the baby behind.

That morning while blessed Elizabeth was in church she called the maid Elizabeth before Matins began and said: "There are a few thalers in my purse which would be of use to that woman with the baby; go and give them to her." When the maid reached the house thinking to find the woman she discovered that the couple had already left leaving the baby alone in the house. She returned and told this to blessed Elizabeth who said: "Go and fetch the baby at once so that she may be cared for." When this was done blessed Elizabeth sent the baby to the wife of a knight who lived in the same village and who would care for her, after which blessed Elizabeth sent for the judge of the place and ordered him to send out messengers to find the mother and bring her back, but they returned after some hours of fruitless search. The maid told this to blessed Elizabeth, begging her to pray that the mother might be found because she was afraid that if Master Conrad happened to hear of the incident it might excite him. Blessed Elizabeth, however, answered her: "I can only pray that God's will may be done." An hour later the husband of the woman appeared and threw himself at Elizabeth's feet saying that he had felt compelled to turn back and could not go on with his wife. He told exactly where the woman was, and a messenger was sent to bring her back and she too confessed that she could not go farther and begged forgiveness for her ingratitude and grave fault. Those standing round were all of the opinion that the cloak and shoes that blessed Elizabeth had given the women should be taken from her and given to someone else, for they said that it was unseemly that a woman of this kind should enjoy blessed Elizabeth's clothes. She however only answered: "Do whatever seems best to you." So the cloak was taken from her and given to a pious girl who at once promised to live in virginity and to serve God as a nun. The shoes were given to a widow; but blessed Elizabeth had pity on the other poor woman and ordered that she should be given another pair of shoes and a fur garment. She then left with the child whom she had formerly so basely deserted.

Irmingarde reported that she had heard blessed Elizabeth say: "The life of the Sisters is what the world most despises; if, however, there were any other life more lowly and contemptible I would choose it. I could have made a vow to some bishop or abbot possessing goods, but I thought it better to make the vow of obedience to Master Conrad who has nothing and is as poor as any beggar because thereby in this life I find no consolation." She also said that she greatly feared Master Conrad since he stood for her as God's representative: "If I am in such dread and awe of a mortal man, how much more I should fear almighty God, who is the Lord and Judge of all."

Irmingarde also told how once Master Conrad had ordered blessed Elizabeth to go to the monastery of Altenberg, and he would there consider whether or not she should remain there. Hearing of her arrival the nuns begged him to allow blessed Elizabeth to enter the enclosure in order that they might see her. He replied: "Let her enter if she wishes to do so," convinced that she would stay outside. Blessed Elizabeth, however, understood his words as a permission for her to enter, and she went in confidently. When Master Conrad heard this he summoned her to come out, and with loud reproaches showed her a book alleging that she had transgressed his order and her vow of obedience and was open to excommunication through having set foot in the enclosure. Although Sister Irmingarde had only stood outside the door he ordered that she should prostrate herself with blessed Elizabeth at his feet because she had held the key and opened the door. He then ordered Brother Gerhard to flagellate them with a long and heavy rod while he sang the *Miserere*. The said Irmingarde added that she had borne the marks of the discipline for three months, and blessed Elizabeth for much longer because she had received much harder blows.

Irmingarde also reported that after blessed Elizabeth had suffered all this she had said: "We must bear such things gladly. We are like a willow growing by the riverside. When a flood comes the willow bends and the water pours over it leaving it undamaged. Then when the flood has passed the willow straightens itself and goes on gladly growing with new strength. And so we too sometimes have to bend down and humble ourselves, and then we rise up strengthened and glad."

Irmingarde also said that blessed Elizabeth was prudent and asked a doctor's advice as to her manner of life in order that she should not overstep the bounds of her strength, and perhaps fall into some illness that would prevent her from serving God, for she dreaded to answer to God for any exaggeration.

Blessed Elizabeth would not allow her maids to call her "Lady" although they were poor and ignorant, and she insisted that they should address her as "Thou Elizabeth." She wished them to sit beside her and eat out of the same dish. Irmingarde once said to her: "You only think of the merit you acquire through us; you do not consider how we may sin through pride because we sit beside you and eat with you." Blessed Elizabeth only replied: "You had best now come and sit on my lap," and this was immediately done.

Irmingarde also told how blessed Elizabeth would wash up the dirty dishes and saucepans and often send away her maids for fear that they should try to hinder her. Repeatedly they found her at this work when they returned or else they found the work already finished. Blessed Elizabeth often visited the poor and sick in their own homes and caused bread, meat, flour, and other victuals to be brought which she distributed to them with her own hands; she also paid much attention to the beds and clothes of the poor. On her return she would fall to prayer and candles were lighted and incense offered and with much devotion she venerated the relics of the saints.

It was her custom to give the poor many presents and when Master Conrad commanded her never to give more than one penny at a time, she took to giving in several times what formerly she had given in a lump sum. Seeing this Master Conrad forbade her to give money, saying she must limit her gifts to bread. This too she gave in installments, but he insisted that she must only give slices of bread and not whole loaves. In all things she was prompt in her obedience to him.

On one occasion when she had started out to visit a hermit Master Conrad sent an order that she should turn back. She answered the messenger with the words: "We are like tortoises who when it rains retire into their shell. So too in order to be obedient let us turn back from the path we had chosen."

She also decreed that her child aged a year and a half should be taken from her in order that she should not love it too much and thereby be hindered in the service of God.

Irmingarde also related that blessed Elizabeth wept most when she was happy and it seemed strange to Irmingarde that anyone should cry and be joyful at the same time. Blessed Elizabeth's face was never distorted or wrinkled by weeping, and the tears flowed down her dear and cheerful face as from a spring leaving her face undisturbed. Of those whose faces were distorted by weeping blessed Elizabeth was wont to say: "It seems as though they wanted to frighten our Lord; they should cheerfully and gladly give God whatever they have."

Once she was in a convent which had no property and lived off daily alms, and the Sisters showed her the paintings in their church and how much gold had been used in the decoration. Blessed Elizabeth turned to the twenty-four Sisters standing around with the words: "Indeed you had much better have spent the money on your clothes and food than on these walls, for you carry these pictures in your hearts." When someone told her of a beautiful picture, wishing to give it to her, she replied: "I do not want any such picture for I carry it in my heart."

In every affliction she was always cheerful and gay, and when any angry or useless words were spoken in her presence she would say: "Where now is our Lord?"

There would be much more that we could say of the sanctity of blessed Elizabeth's life, of her humility, patience, simplicity which has been reported to us by those who lived in close contact with her. In order to avoid prolixity we will only here add something about her death.

The above mentioned maid of the Lady Elizabeth related as follows.

"When my lady, blessed Elizabeth, lay on her death bed I heard a sweet voice which came from her throat. She was lying turned to the wall, but after an hour she turned over saying: 'Where are you, dear?' I answered: 'O my Lady, how sweetly you were singing,' and she asked me whether I too had heard the song. When I assured her that I had she said: 'I tell you that between me and the wall there was a little bird singing most merrily, and its voice made me sing too.' This was several days before she died."

The same maid declared: "My Lady, blessed Elizabeth, always spoke to us her maids with cheerful words, calling us her dear ones and her friends.

"As we stood round the bed where she lay dying she said: 'What should we do were the devil to appear?' Rather later, as though she were repulsing him she called out loudly: 'Fly, fly, fly,' adding: 'Now let us talk of God and of His Son Jesus; it is already night and near the hour when Jesus was born and lay in the crib. And His almighty power had created a new star hitherto unseen by anyone.' At these words she became so cheerful as though she were not ill, and she said: 'Though I am weak I have not any pain.'"

The maid Irmingarde told us that she had heard blessed Elizabeth say shortly before she died: "Now the hour has come for God to call His friends." She said that during that whole day she had been filled with great devotion, and even when she died she seemed to be quietly sleeping and so gently breathed out her spirit.

Although the body of blessed Elizabeth remained four days

ST. ELIZABETH RECEIVES
THE HABIT OF THE
THIRD ORDER

ELIZABETH GIVING ALMS

(Both pictures from the reliquary which contained her body. Marburg, Marburg Kunstinstitut.)

SAINT ELIZABETH

Simone Martini
Lower Church of St. Francis. Assisi.

GENERAL VIEW OF MARBURG

hic pater & natus, hic est & spe alinus.

A Page From the Psalter
of St. Elizabeth in Cividale
With Portraits of Herman
and Sophie of Thuringia

Cross Said to Have Been
Sent to St. Elizabeth by
Pope Gregory IX
Preserved in the Monastery
of Andechs

unburied, it emitted no unpleasant odor as is generally the case, but rather a most sweet scent refreshing the spirit of all. She had on her gray habit, a linen cloth round her head; as she lay there many out of devotion cut off bits of the stuff and even her hair and nails. Certain women took bits from her ears and even the nipples of her breasts were cut off as relics. It is hard to describe the paroxysms of grief of individuals, the cries of sorrow of the crowds of poor who came streaming in to weep over the death of her who had become the mother of all. After the Dirge had been prayed the abbess of Wetter who was present heard the song of birds, and wishing to ascertain where they were she went outside the church and saw a great company of birds assembled round the tower as though they too were participating in the Office.

We have heard a great more about the life and piety of blessed Elizabeth and we could have reported at far greater length about her hospital in Marburg and of her most praiseworthy care of the sick and poor in this hospital, and of all the silken and purple coverings therein, but wishing to avoid verbosity we have only allowed extracts of all this to be noted down.

LETTERS OF CONRAD OF MARBURG TO POPE GREGORY IX

First Letter Relating to the Miracles

Raymond Abbot of Eberbach of the Cistercian Order and Master Conrad of Marburg, preacher of the word of God, to the Holy Father Gregory, and to Siegfried Archpriest of the Roman Church and through God's grace Archbishop of Mainz, with deep devotion, childlike obedience, and the profoundest reverence.

We have received the Letter of Your Paternity with the commission to inform you of all that we, ever mindful of God's majesty, have discovered regarding the behavior and life of the former Landgräfin Elizabeth of blessed memory, and regarding the wonders which God works through her holy body. In obedience to this apostolic commission we have made inquiries from suitable witnesses and have noted down their testimony with careful zeal and alert attention in writings which bearing our seals we now forward by the hands of reliable and trustworthy messengers.

Obedient to your order as was our bounden duty we have done our utmost with zealous care to discover everything concerning the life of the said Landgräfin and concerning the wonders worked by God through her holy body; this we have recorded in the document we now send to Your Holiness.

We have interrogated her God-fearing and pious servants about her life after having prudently put them on oath, and we have noted in writing what they have told us. I, the humble preacher Conrad, have taken it down word for word intending it for Your eye; and in conscience none of us has heard anything that might have led us to change, or to eliminate anything that has been said, nor to add anything further to it.

Second Letter of Master Conrad of Marburg to the Pope Concerning the Life of Blessed Elizabeth

It is surely known to You Holy Father that Your Penitentiary Brother Raymond has written to me several times instructing me to inform you concerning the wonders worked by God through the Lady Elizabeth, formerly Landgräfin of Thuringia, whom Your Holiness had entrusted to my care and protection. I therefore took the opportunity offered on the last feast of Saint Laurence when the Lord Archbishop of Mainz had come on my entreaty to consecrate two altars in the basilica where lies the body of the above-named Elizabeth. A great concourse of people had gathered there at my instigation and during the sermon without any previous consultation I wished to fulfill Your Holiness' command by obtaining the testimony of all present about the forenamed wonders and the cures obtained through the merits of the Landgräfin. Therefore I summoned all these people to appear early the next day before the Archbishop of Mainz and other prelates gathered here for the ceremony that they should bear sworn witness to the graces obtained through the invocation of the Lady Elizabeth. In answer to my invitation a large crowd presented themselves declaring they had been healed of their ills through Elizabeth; the Archbishop of Mainz was in a hurry having other important business to attend to, and therefore he caused only the most striking of these healings to be noted down appending his own seal to the document and that of other prelates. The confirmation of many of the prelates and other important persons was not recorded since they had no seal with them.

In order that Your Holiness should not only hear of these miracles I will now give you an account of her life.

I was her confessor for two years before her husband's death. When she was entrusted to my direction, she complained to me that she was bound by matrimony and could not end her earthly life as a virgin. During the time that her husband was with the Emperor in Apulia Germany was suffering through a terrible famine, and many people died of hunger. Elizabeth already then shone with many virtues; throughout her life she was the consoler of the poor, and she began to feed the hungry and built a hospital near her castle where she gave shelter to many children and ill folk. She gave copious victuals to all who came to beg for alms. She did this not only in that place, but in all her husband's principalities where she used up the reserves of corn and finally sold her jewels and rich clothes for the benefit of the poor.

She was in the habit of visiting her sick twice a day in person, in the morning and evening; she nursed the most repulsive cases herself, fed many with her own hands, served them, and carried them about and did much else for them. In all this she had her husband's approval.

When her husband died and Your Holiness entrusted her to my care she was striving for the highest perfection and asked me whether she would have more merit serving God as a hermit, in a monastery, or in any other state. Her dominating desire was that I should allow her to beg from door to door, and with many tears she implored me to consent. When I roughly forbade it she answered: "Then I will do what you cannot prevent," and on Good Friday, when the altars were stripped in the church she had given to the Friars Minor, and in the presence of several friars she laid her hands on the altar and renounced her parents and children, her own will, and all worldly pomp and everything which our Lord in the Gospel counsels us to give up.

After this, against my will, she followed me to Marburg on the frontier of her husband's domains for she feared the enticements of the restless world, and of remaining in the place where during her husband's life she had played a considerable part. In Marburg she built a hospital in which she gathered the sick, the poor, and set the most humble and miserable at her own table. When I reproved her for this she answered that it brought her special graces of humility, and referring to her past life, like the clever woman she was, she insisted that for her it was necessary to heal one extreme through its opposite extreme. When I saw her so set on spiritual progress I removed all her superfluous servants, and bade her to be content with three persons, a lay brother to see to her business matters, an unattractive girl, and a very severe widow, in order that the girl should try her humility and the repulsive widow her patience.

While the girl was washing the cabbage her mistress washed the dishes, and vice versa. Among others she took in a paralyzed orphan boy who suffered continually from dysentery. In order to exercise herself in perfection she put him to sleep in her bed, suffering many things through him, for often six times and even more in the night she would carry him to satisfy his natural wants. She washed his dirty linen cloths with her own hands.

When the boy died, without my knowledge she took in a leper girl, hid her in the house and served her in every way. She would feed her, make her bed, wash her, take off her shoes, humbling herself in many ways, and cleverly won her servants' silence by begging them not to get her into trouble with me. When I did hear of it, may God forgive me, I gave her a sound beating because I feared she might catch the disease and I took the leper girl away from her.

While I was away preaching she took in a poor boy covered with scurvy whose head was in such a state that he hardly had a hair left; she treated him with medicines, washed him, and did all to cure him. This boy was sitting by her bed when she died.

Besides all this before God I declare that I have seldom found a woman more given to contemplation. Monks and nuns often saw how her face was wonderfully illuminated when she came from prayer and her eyes shone with rays of sun. When, as often happened, she was for hours in ecstasy, after it she took no, or hardly any food.

Finally when she was near death, but still apparently quite well, I was troubled by a severe illness and asked her how she would manage her life after my death. She answered by fore-telling her own death without the slightest hesitation. On the fourth day after this conversation she fell ill, and continued so for twelve days. Three days before her death she would not see any secular persons including those nobles who often came to see her. When these asked why they were shut out she said to those around her that she wished to think of the Last Things, of the Judgment and God the almighty Judge. On the Sunday before the octave of the Feast of Saint Martin she made her confession to me, but could think of nothing beyond those things she had already often confessed. When I asked her what was to be done with her belongings and furniture she answered that everything which appeared to be hers belonged to the poor, and begged me to divide up these things with the exception of the old worn cloak in which she was wrapped and in which she wished to be buried.

When this was over very early she received our Lord's body, and until Vespers she spoke of passages in sermons that had struck her, and especially of the raising of Lazarus, and how on that occasion our Lord had wept. This caused several monks and nuns who were present to weep but she said: "Daughters of Jerusalem, weep not for me, but for yourselves." After this she was silent, and though her lips did not move, a sweet song came from her throat and when those sitting by her bed asked what it might be, she asked if they had not heard someone sing-ing with her. From twilight onward she lay there full of gladness and showing complete resignation until the first cockcrow, at which she said: "See the hour is at hand when the Virgin gave birth to her Son." Then she humbly commended all with her to God and quietly passed into sleep.

On hearing of her death Cistercian monks and Brothers of

other Orders came from many places to the hospital where she was to be buried. The devotion of the people demanded that she should remain unburied until the fourth weekday, and except for her paleness she showed no sign of death, and her body was as flexible as it had been in life. From it there emanated a most sweet scent. On the day after her burial the Lord began to work miracles through His handmaiden, for a Cistercian monk at her tomb was healed of the madness which had afflicted him for forty years and he swore to this before me and the parish priest of Marburg.

There follow the miracles of holy Elizabeth.

EXTRACTS FROM THE DEPOSITION CONCERNING THE MIRACLES

THE RECORD of the miracles sent to Rome for the canonization of Elizabeth is extraordinarily vivid; we really seem to be standing by watching and listening as the pitiable cases approach the place where Elizabeth lies buried. We see every form of suffering, and the anxiety of those who bring their children, their parents, their friends to be healed. Elizabeth *must* help; since God has seen fit to take away the one person on whom the most miserable and abject could always count, He *must* open some way for the relief of their suffering. And the way was opened and Elizabeth did not fail. The invocation is nearly always the same: "Blessed Lady, help me, make my child see, make her walk, heal me, let me hear." One seems to be listening to the invocations of Lourdes. "Saint Elizabeth, here is my son, I give him to you, only heal him"; "Blessed Lady, pity me, deliver me from my torment so as to oblige me always to serve thee." Some of the pilgrims promise an annual visit to Elizabeth's tomb, they bring offerings of money, and candles occasionally the sufferer's weight in wax, silver, or corn. Some of the cures occur immediately after making a vow actually at the tomb, sometimes on the journey back, and even at home. The number of ex-votos, generally waxen figures, hanging round the tomb increase; the hospital attendants are kept busy providing for the needs of the pilgrims; many of the details are so realistic that we seem to smell what the onlookers smelled, see the poor deformed, disfigured sufferers, many covered with sores, notice one woman in vain trying to keep the flies off her child's inflamed eyes, hear the cries of the mad, the imploring invocations of the relations and friends, and again the jubilant thanksgiving, the sobs of gratitude. Often the sufferer is placed near the tomb, is sometimes brought there two, three, four times, and trust is subjected to the test of a long wait. Over and over again the commissioners listened to the same words: "We saw so and so, paralyzed, blind, full of sores, demented, crippled, and then we saw him cured." The testimony had to be direct: more than half the recorded miracles were on children, and in the two sessions of 1233 and 1235 some 130 cases were submitted to Rome. Here are a few examples:

"Wigard of Mederbach of the Cologne diocese, when asked about the death of Gottfried, a four-year-old child, affirmed on oath that on coming to draw water from a well he found the child submerged, having fallen in. Much alarmed he quickly descended, picked up the child handing him to his companion who had also come to draw water. Their shouts brought other folk hurrying from the village and all saw that the child was dead; his mouth was open, his eyes horribly staring, his skin black and wrinkled as boiled in scalding water, his belly extremely swollen, his arms and legs, all his limbs completely rigid. The child was taken to Wigard's house and no word was sent to the parents, for the father was ill and the mother in childbirth. All present earnestly prayed to Saint Elizabeth for help, and two devout women were told to make a vow to take the child to the saint's tomb with the customary offerings. As soon as the vow had been pronounced the child's color began to return, and his pulse could be felt, so then he was carried to his parents' house.

"Rüdiger, who had come with Wigard to draw water, said on oath that he took the child from Wigard still standing in the well from which he had lifted the child. He, Rüdiger, laid the child on the ground weeping because he thought it was his son whom he had last seen perfectly well; the child was so disfigured that he could not recognize it. On all other points he agreed with Wigard.

"Wipert, the child's father, and Gertrude, his mother, affirmed on oath that on Saint John the Baptist's Day of this present year about the hour of Vespers little Gottfried had left the house to play with other children; they did not know at what hour he fell into the well, but about sunset he was brought back to them. Adelheid of the same village affirmed on oath that she saw the child lying inanimate on the ground and everyone crying. We the commissioners saw the child alive and well." (No. 10 of the 1233 deposition, repeated in that of 1235.)

"Mathilde of Biedenkopf, of the diocese of Mainz, aged fifty, affirmed on oath that she had been blind in her left eye for three years. Having heard of the miracles done by God through the intercession of blessed Elizabeth she made a vow and taking with her some offerings she went to the chapel where the lady Saint Elizabeth was buried. Presenting her humble gifts she implored the lady Elizabeth that through her merits God might restore her sight. At once instantaneously sight returned to her left eye, but her right eye was completely blinded. When she returned home she recounted the miracle of how she had recovered the sight of one eye, and lost that of the other at which many people laughed, but she cried. As she was returning to the tomb to give testimony as to what had happened she heard people singing a German song about the sad parting of blessed Elizabeth from her husband, the Landgraf Ludwig, when he set out for the Crusade. This song so moved Mathilde that she began to cry bitterly and while she wept her sight was completely restored and she saw perfectly with both eyes.

"Asked when she had recovered the sight in the first eye she answered: 'On the day of Saint Michael'; asked when the sight returned to the second eye she answered: 'On the eve of the Epiphany of this year.'

"Adelheid, her daughter Hildegunde, Hadewige and Hellenburge all of the same place affirmed on oath that they had often

heard her lament about her blindness and they believed that
she was telling the truth." (No. 84 of the 1233 deposition, repeated in that of 1235.)

"Isentrude of Schletzenrod, of the diocese of Mainz, affirmed
on oath that her son Dietrich aged five was born blind, with
no sign of eyes in his face. From his birth the eye socket was
completely covered with skin like the rest of his body with no
eyelids. Asked how and when he began to see, she answered:
'On Holy Thursday of this year'; asked where this happened,
she answered: 'At the right hand corner of the hospital chapel
where the princess Elizabeth is buried.' Asked how it came
about, she answered: 'During the sermon in the open air the
skin which hitherto had completely covered the eyes seemed as
though it had been slit with a knife and the eyes appeared,
very small, very mobile like tadpoles one sees in water, and
blood shot.' Asked what invocation she had made, she answered:
'I prayed to Saint Elizabeth' adding that she had taken earth
from the tomb and rubbed it on the child's face. . . . Ludwig
of Linsingen, a knight, on oath confirmed that as he was on
his way to hear the sermon of Master Conrad he saw this
woman sitting in the chapel and crying bitterly. He asked the
cause of her distress and she answered that it was on account
of her child born blind. Asked whether he had seen the child's
face, he answered that he had not on account of the crowd
pressing round, but when asked what he knew of the child he
said that he saw the child directly after the sermon and no
longer blind. The eyes appeared to have been slit, the eyes
were very small, watering, and without eyelashes. Wishing to
prove whether the child could see he offered him a coin and
then threw it into a pot. The child stretched out his hand and
picked out the coin.

"Cunegonde of Schletzenrod, aunt of the child, and her son
Conrad affirmed on oath that they had seen the child blind
throughout a year with skin covering the eye sockets so that
the eyes were completely hidden, but since the last Holy Thurs-

day they had observed that he saw perfectly well with clear eyes. Asked why they had only seen him blind for one year, they answered that the mother with her little boy lived in another place. We who took down the evidence of the witnesses saw for ourselves that the child saw clearly with eyes of normal size.

"Lutrude of Röddenau, of the diocese of Mainz, affirmed on oath that this year (1232) about the time of the Feast of Saint James she found her son Wezelin, aged about three and a half, dead. His body had been inanimate and rigid for something like the time it takes to go four German miles; she caught up the child and crying and screaming carried him into the courtyard calling on the neighbors that they might come and prepare the grave clothes and whatever else was necessary for the burial according to the custom of that place. While the neighboring women were coming she cried out loudly: 'Blessed Elizabeth, why have I lost my child? Come to my help, let his spirit come back into him and I will lay him on thy tomb together with the weight of his body in bread, corn, incense, myrrh, linen, silver, and wax.' Very soon after she had said these words the child's life returned and the first sign was the renewed pulsation of his arteries. From that moment which was toward sunset the child could utter no sound until the middle of the night when he exclaimed three times: 'Darling, where am I?' Until then he had not recognized his mother, and his strength only returned gradually. When asked as to the length of the illness preceding the child's death, his mother answered that he had been ill for five days. Irmentrude of the same village, and neighbor of the woman, affirmed on oath that while she was watering her garden she heard the screams of this woman who was well known to her. She hastened to go to her thinking that some misfortune had happened to the child whom she knew to be ill. When she reached the house she found the woman outside holding the child in her arms; he was inanimate, his eyes wide open and fixed, absolutely without any movement, exactly like a corpse. With the child's mother she began to invoke blessed

Elizabeth. She left the mother with the child still inanimate, having to return to her own house where she too had an ill person; after a short time she heard voices calling out in joy that the child's life had been restored.

"Conrad, of the same village, affirmed on oath that hearing the mother's cries he ran to her with other people, and saw the child on her knees and took him for dead. He agreed with the other witnesses as to the time and place. And we who listened to these witnesses saw with our own eyes that the child is alive and healthy.

"Gertrude, a girl of the diocese of Trier, affirmed on oath that for three years she had been blind in one eye and therefore her father and mother made a vow to take her to the tomb of blessed Elizabeth in Marburg, and the sight returned to her eye before even she had arrived there.

"Petrissa, mother of this same girl, affirmed on oath that she had entered the oratory of blessed Francis in Marburg and invoked his help together with that of blessed Elizabeth; she made a vow to bring her daughter to Marburg and while they were still on the way, before reaching the sanctuary, her daughter's eye was healed as has been already said.

"Ortwinus, of the same place, affirmed on oath that he had seen the girl when she was blind in one eye, and was firmly convinced that her sight had been restored through the merits of blessed Elizabeth. Adelheid, of the same place, on oath made the same affirmation."

This last miracle is the only instance where the name of Francis is coupled with that of Elizabeth. Irmentrude, wife of the director of the Marburg hospital, was a witness of two miracles, together with Irmingarde who is described as custodian of blessed Elizabeth's tomb. On one occasion the miracle was on a man who had been lame for more than twenty years with a shortened leg which caused him much pain and when giving evidence he stressed the effort he had made and his great diffi-culty in reaching Marburg from Mainz whereas he returned home walking gladly and easily. The other miracle was on a girl of thirteen who was humpbacked and entirely crippled. Two of her thigh bones had pierced through her skin and in this state she was brought to Marburg and remained near the tomb of blessed Elizabeth for eleven weeks. Gradually her bones went back into place, her limbs were straightened and the girl went home entirely cured and with no sign of any deformity.

The maid Elizabeth who with the lay brother Heinrich is described as custodian of the tomb witnessed the miracle on a three-year-old child who had never been able to walk. His mother was crying bitterly when they reached the tomb and was urged by Brother Heinrich to lay the child down beside it, invoking blessed Elizabeth. Brother Heinrich then showed the child an egg, and slowly the child got up stretching out his hand; as the Brother moved from one end of the tomb to the other, the child followed him holding on to the tomb still looking at the egg which the Brother held out in front of him and his walking power became assured.

THE CAUSE AND ORDER OF CANONIZATION OF BLESSED ELIZABETH

THE following account is preserved with the record of the miracles, the relation of the Four Servants, and the Letters of Conrad of Marburg. It is of interest in that it shows how a medieval canonization was conducted; it was drawn up to counteract contemporary "calumny and detraction" and it may have been written by the Pope's Confessor, Raymond of Penafort, the Dominican who is also one of the Church's saints.

When the fame of the Servant of God blessed Elizabeth together with the news of the wonders worked by God through her spread far and wide with increasing insistence so that it reached the Apostolic See, our Holy Father Gregory IX, to whom is entrusted the apostolic care of all the churches, declared the need for prudence in this matter. As is the duty of the watchful shepherd he did this to ward off the danger of error and to protect truth so that the pious simplicity of the Church Militant should not be deceived by any discrepancy between fact and rumor, and also to insure that the praise of the Church Triumphant and the thanksgiving due to the Creator of all things should not suffer were the rumor really ascertained to be substantiated by truth. Therefore the Holy Father ordered the worthy Bishop Conrad of Hildesheim and the abbots Ludwig of Hersfeld and Raymond of Eberbach, all men of great experience and the last two members of a religious order, to go in person to that place in Marburg which claims to be the scene of the far-famed wonders, and there to summon suitable witnesses who in the customary sacramental form should recount on oath what was known to them concerning the life of the blessed Servant of God Elizabeth. They were then within a given time to forward the findings of their inquiry sealed with their own seals, to the Papal Curia. In the same manner other reliable witnesses were to be interrogated as to the miracles, in order to establish firstly that the person in question appeared to be really ill, and that after the invocation of God, and the invocation of blessed Elizabeth, either an immediate recovery had occurred or that the sufferer had been greatly helped toward restored health, but that in either case the improvement was only due to the invocation, and not to any gradual recovery of natural strength or to the use of medicines. The points were to be established as a test of the reality of the miracles.

In obedience to the apostolic commission the aforenamed Bishop designated a day on which those who had experienced the Lord's mercy or had personal knowledge of the occurrence, after being identified by their parish priest and the prelates of Marburg, should then appear before him in order to give evidence of the truth, and he published this summons in all the archbishoprics and dioceses according to the authority of his office.

On the appointed day many thousands of people from all parts assembled for this purpose with many Cistercian abbots, priors and brothers of the Dominicans and of the Franciscans, the monks of Saint Norbert, the Canons Regular as well as Secular Canons, the Brothers of the Teutonic Order, and many learned and clever men whose names and offices were later communicated to the Holy Father. All these received the Sacrament to the strengthening of their duty to speak only and nothing but the truth, neither adding to it nor detracting from it, after which the other articles of Canon Law were read aloud. The Lord Bishop then carefully heard the witnesses and caused what they said to be written down faithfully by lawyers, the documents being then sealed with his own seal and that of the abbots, his fellow officials, and also the seals of many other prelates who were present. After this it was entrusted to the Abbot Bernard of Buch, the preacher, Master Solomon, and the former Landgraf of Thuringia, Brother Conrad of the Teutonic Order, all honorable and reliable men with the order that they, accompanied by a number of monks, should convey the document to the Holy See.

Besides the aforenamed Bishop and the abbots his companions, many other archbishops, bishops, abbots, superiors of religious orders, prelates, dukes, markgraves and secular princes and nobles of both sexes belonging to the Holy German Kingdom notified our Holy Father the Pope concerning the matter in hand dealing with its truth, with the circumstances, stating what was alleged by public opinion, and what were the real ascertained facts; they recounted what had actually been seen, heard, proved, and experienced, and in the same letter humbly begged that the Holy Father would not allow this shining example of charity to be hidden under a bushel, or be stifled by the pressure of heretics for the Just, All-knowing Judge in heaven had already allowed magnificent and public proof of Elizabeth's sanctity to be forthcoming. Since, therefore, the judgment of man should, as far as is possible, follow that of God they prayed the Holy Father that the Church Militant should honor what is honored by the Church Triumphant, and that all mankind should unite their homage to that of the citizens of heaven, so that what is the joy of the angelic choirs should also stimulate the devotion of the faithful.

After the matter had been subjected to a most exhaustive and detailed examination it was firmly and clearly established that the Divine Wisdom had drawn blessed Elizabeth from the storms and floods of sorrow to the shore of eternal rest. The report of the witnesses was read and commented on by a Consistory in the presence of the Holy Father Gregory, the Patriarchs of Antioch and Jerusalem, the Cardinals who govern the Church and illumine her and their own countries by their wisdom and bring peace to the peoples. There were also present many archbishops, bishops, and different prelates, besides a large number of priests and monks who, when they had heard the evidence unanimously declared blessed Elizabeth worthy to be set on the beacon of apostolic canonization, and to be inscribed on earth in the Book of the Saints since it is beyond doubt that her name is written in the Book of Life by God's own marvelous decree.

On the Feast of Pentecost the Holy Father Gregory with all the aforesaid prelates and many thousands of the faithful went in solemn procession to the sound of trumpets and horns to the church of the Friars Preachers where the above-mentioned Brother Conrad, formerly the Landgraf, who was lovingly acclaimed by all, presented enormous decorated candles to the Pope, to the prelates and monks, and also candles to the whole concourse which were afterward given to the said Church.

The Cardinal Deacon thereupon announced to the assembly all concerning the life and miracles of blessed Elizabeth which was received with general acclamation and many tears and while the sweet melody of the solemn singing of the Hymn of Angels rose to heaven, Elizabeth was solemnly declared to be a saint, a woman blessed among all, and worthy of all praise. The day of her death was decreed to be kept as her feast, and the Lord Pope then pronounced the Collect and Secret and other parts of the Mass which he himself had composed. Then, thanking God for all His mercies, those present returned to their own homes.

The said Brother Conrad invited some three hundred priests to dinner and sent gifts to many different convents and provided bread, wine, fish, and cheese for many hermits, recluses, and Poor Sisters of Saint Francis. Besides this he gave bread, meat, wine, and money to many thousands of poor in the name of the Teutonic Order, to the honor of God. This greatly pleased the Lord Pope, who since Brother Conrad's arrival had shown him every favor and now invited him to dine at his own table and to sit at his side, and this happens very seldom. Brother Conrad's followers were also suitably entertained and then most graciously dismissed. All the petitions of the poor which had been sent to the Curia presented by Brother Conrad were graciously accorded and the Holy Father blessed him with many tears and kissed him and took an affectionate farewell of him.

The Holy Father sent many Letters not only to the States of the Church, but to every kingdom and every archbishopric in which he announced what is here recorded together with his sincere love desiring that what He had written should be taken note of and observed.

Written in Perugia in the Year of Our Lord 1235.

THE BULL OF CANONIZATION

From His place in the glory of the eternal Father, our Redeemer Jesus Christ saw the misery of our human condition in that moral deformity caused by the sin of our first parents. Moved by compassion, God's ineffable Providence decreed that our human nature, the work of His hands, should experience His omnipotent mercy, and by Him be freed from the shadow of death and called back to the fatherland of divine liberty. Thus the Creator in His infinite Wisdom willed to perfect the work He had begun and to restore the fallen creature to its pristine dignity. To this end He entered the narrow womb of the Virgin (if that can be called narrow which harbors in itself the Lord who contains all things) and leaving His royal throne He took upon Himself our nature, He who is invisible made Himself visible, and through the mystery of His Incarnation and the triumph of His Redemption He defeated the Prince of Darkness and all his works, and thereby He opened to His faithful followers a sure way by which they might return to their eternal home.

Blessed Elizabeth of royal lineage and the gracious Landgräfin of Thuringia gave herself to earnest meditation on the mystery of our Redemption; and this continued from her earliest years to the end of her life. Above all else she desired to become worthy of eternal glory and devoted herself to the consistent practice of virtue following the path traced by our Lord Jesus Christ, and she never ceased to find joy in the embrace of charity. Always confessing the true faith she dedicated herself to a life of sanctity inspired by love for the Divine Son of the Queen of Heaven, the divine Bridegroom of her soul, and she had such love for her neighbor that she wished to have near her those whose condition caused them to be generally shunned. She became voluntarily poor in many things in order to be rich toward those in need; from her earliest age she always wished to be their protector and friend knowing that the reward of eternal life is to be acquired by the merits of God's friends the poor. She came so to love this condition which is despised by worldly pride that she repeatedly showed her contempt for even those legitimate pleasures open to her through the exalted rank of her husband, and mortifying her delicate body by the constant practice of renunciation she progressed in virtue to the point where a spontaneous action of self-denial is rewarded by more abundant grace. What more can be said? In her desire for the highest happiness after her husband's death she set aside all family ties considering it as an imperfection did she not obediently remain in a state of chastity; indeed she had already made a vow to this end during her husband's lifetime, only excepting his just claims upon her. As a widow, therefore, she put on the religious habit in which until her death she continued to live the mystery of Christ's passion.

O blessed wife! O marvelous woman! O sweet Elizabeth whose very name signifies one filled and satisfied with God, and who by feeding the poor hast merited the bread of Angels! O glorious widow, rich in virtues, who sought to obtain through grace what nature cannot give; thou didst triumph over the soul's cruel enemies by the shield of faith, the armour of justice, the sword of the Spirit, the helmet of salvation, and the spear of perseverance! Elizabeth endeared herself to the immortal Bridegroom by unflagging love, and reducing her earthly dignity to the humble office of a servant she was united to the Queen of Virgins; she made herself like the saints of other times by following uncomplainingly God's laws and commandments, and by grace conceived God in her inmost soul, bringing Him to birth in her actions, feeding Him by her unceasing progress to such a point that the Lord who is the only support of those who hope in Him, who exalts the humble and innocent, arose to bestow on her the reward promised to His followers and delivered her from the bond of death and has carried her to the throne of the elect in the dwelling of inaccessible light.

This astonishing and ineffable transfiguration has caused her spirit to shine in the infinity of the divine light and its rays reach into the abyss of our darkness by the glorious miracles that increase the faith, hope, and charity of the faithful, show the way to those who have strayed from the way of truth. Heretics are confounded in the depths of their estrangement when they see the dead brought back to life, sight being given to the blind, hearing to the deaf, speech to the dumb, the power of walking to the infirm, and vast regions of Germany which they had thought to poison with their doctrines turning with joy to the divine teaching of our Lord. All this comes to pass by the divine grace working through the merits of this saint who while on earth showed herself poor in spirit, unfailingly tender of heart, bewailing her sins, or rather those of others, thirsting for righteousness, given to mercy, pure of heart, truly peace loving, bearing persecution and opprobrium with serenity.

These stupendous events have been irrefutably attested; and We have consulted Our Brothers the venerable Patriarchs, Archbishops, Bishops, and Prelates of Our court, it being incumbent on us to watch carefully over all that may contribute to the glory of our Redeemer. This being done We have inscribed the name of Elizabeth in the catalogue of the Saints, and order that her feast shall be celebrated on the thirteenth day of the calends of December, being the day on which the bonds of death were broken and she flew to the Fountainhead of supreme joy, so that through her intercession we too with Christ's help may obtain what she has already obtained and now glories in its eternal possession. Furthermore availing ourselves of the power conferred on Us by God who wills that all the faithful should share in the divine graces, We desire that God's Holy Name should be honored by numerous pilgrims to the venerable tomb of His bride Elizabeth, and trusting in His mercy and by the authority of the blessed Apostles Peter and Paul we grant one year and forty days' Indulgence to all those who, having confessed their sins with true contrition, shall visit this sanctuary on the day of the feast or during the octave, there to offer their prayers and devotion.

Given at Perugia in the calends of June in the ninth year of Our Pontificate.

BIBLIOGRAPHY

This does not include details of manuscripts in various libraries, but only the works in which they can be studied.

Ancelet-Hustache, Jeanne, *Sainte Elisabeth d'Hongrie* (Editions Franciscaines [Paris: 1946]).

Basnage, Jacob, *Theodorici Ruringi, Ordinis Praedicatorum, libri octo de S. Elisabeth.* . . . *Editi ex m.s.; membris Monasterii S. Magni ad pedem pontis Ratispoenensis*, pp. 113–152.

—— *Thesaurus Monumentorum ecclesiasticorum et historicorum sive Henrici Canisii lectiones antiquae, Ad Saeculorum digestae variisque opusculis auctae quibus praefationes historicas, animadversiones criticas, et nota in singulos auctores adjecit*, Tomus IV (Antwerp: 1725).

Boerner, Gustav, *Zur Crikik der Quellen für die Geschichte der heiligen Elisabeth (Neues Archiv der Gesellschaft fur ältere deutsche Geschichtskunde* [1888]).

Bücking, R., *Geschichtliche Bilder aus Marburgs Vergangenheit* (1901).

Cambridge Medieval History, Vols. IV and V.

Chérancé, Fr. Léopold de, *Sainte Elisabeth d'Hongrie* (1917).

Clifton, Violet, *Sanctity*.

Doelle, Ferdinand, *Die Franziskaner in Deutschland*.

Giebesbrecht, W. von, *Geschichte der Deutschen Kaiserseit* (1881).

Gorres-Coudenhove, Ida Frederike, *Gespräch uber die Heiligkeit, ein Dialog um Elisabeth von Thüringen* (1931).

Grousset, René, *Histoire des Croisades et du Royaume Franc de Jérusalem* (Paris: 1936).

Haseloff, Arthur, *Eine Thuringisch-Sächsische Malerschule des 13ten Jahrhunderts* (Strassburg: 1897).

—— *Die Glasgemälde der Elisabethenkirche in Marburg*.

Holder-Egger, Oswald, *Monumenta Germaniae Historica*, Script. XXX (1896).

Horn, Emile, *Sainte Elisabeth d'Hongrie* (Paris: 1902).

Huyskens, Albert, *Quellenstudien zur Geschichte der heiligen Elisabeth, Landgräfin von Thüringen* (Marburg: 1908).

———— "Des Cäsärius von Heisterbach, Schriften uber die heilige Elisabeth von Thüringen" (Annalem des historischen Vereins fur den Niederrein [Köln: 1908]).

———— Der sogenannte Libellus de Dictis Quatuor Ancillarum S. Elisabeth confectus (München: 1911).

———— Der Hospitalbau der heiligen Elisabeth und die erste Wallfarhtskirche zu Marburg (Zeitschrift des Vereins fur Hessische Geschichtskunde [Kassel: 1909]).

———— Die Heilige Elisabeth. Lexikon fur Theologie und Kirche (1931).

Jano, Fr. Jordani, O.M., Chronica (Analecta Francescana, I).

Jubinal, Achille, Oeuvres Completes de Rutebeuf . . . La Vie Sainte Elysabet (Paris: 1839).

Justi, K. W., Elisabeth die heilige Landgräfin von Thüringen (Zurich: 1797).

Kantorowicz, Friedrich II (1927).

Kopke, Fr. Karl, Das Passional, eine Legendensammlung des dreizehnten Jahrhundert (Quedlinborg und Leipzig: 1852).

Lemmens, P. I., Zur Biographie der heiligen Elisabeth, Landgräfin von Thüringen (Mitteilungen des historischen Vereins der Diozese Fulda [1901]).

Liliencron, R. von, Düringische Chronik des Johann Rothe (Jena: 1859).

Maresch, Dr. Maria, Elisabeth von Thüringen (Buchgemeinde, Bonn: 1931).

Mielke, Hellmuth, Zur Biographie der heiligen Elisabeth (1888), Rostock.

———— Die heilige Elisabeth, Landgräfin von Thüringen (Sammlung gemeinverstandlicher wissenshaftlicher Vortrage, Neue Folge, VI [Hamburg: 1892]).

Mihalik, Alessandro, Gioielli di Sant'Elisabetta d'Ungheria a Udine ed a Cividale (Miscellanea Francescana [1936]).

Montalembert, Comte de, Histoire de Sainte Elisabeth de Hongrie, duchesse de Thuringe (Paris: 1836).

Potthast, Augustus, Regesta Pontificium Romanorum (Berlin: 1874).

Rieger, Max, Das Leben der heiligen Elisabeth vom Verfasser der Erlösung (Stuttgart: 1866).

Ruckert, Heinrich, Das Leben des heiligen Ludwig Landgrafen von Thüringen Gemahls der heiligen Elisabeth nach der Lateinischen Urschrift ubersetzt von Friedrich Ködiz von Salfeld (Leipzig: 1851).

Schmidt-Pauli, Elisabeth von, *Pilgerin auf Erden. Leben der heiligen Elisabeth* (Verlag fur Kultur politik, Berlin: 1931).

Stein, Edith, *Lebenstaltung im Geist der heiligen Elisabeth;* in *Frauenbildung und Frauenberufe* (1949).

Strauss-Tourney, Luke von, *Das Leben der heiligen Elizabeth nach alten Quellen erzählt* (Jena: 1925).

Voragine, Jacobus de, *Legenda Aurea; the Golden Legend,* November 19, translated into English by William Caxton. New Edition Temple Classics (Dent: 1931).

Wadding, L., *Annales Minorum* (Quaracchi: 1931).

Weinrich, Franz Johannes, *Elisabeth von Thüringen* (Munich: 1949).

Wenck, Karl, *Die Enstehung der Reinhardsbrunner Gesichtsbucher* (Halle: 1878).

——— *Zur Entstehungschichte der Reinhardsbrunner Historien und der Erfurter Peterschronik* (*Neues Archiv der Gesellschaft fur ältere deutsche Geschichtskunde* [1885]).

——— *Ludwig der Heilige, Landgraf von Thüringen* (*Allgemeine Deutsche Biographie* [Leipzig: 1884]). *"Alteste Geschichte der Wartburg"; "Die heilige Elisabeth"; "Geschichte der Landgrafen und der Wartburg als fürstlicher Residenz."* These last three articles appeared in *Die Wartburg, ein Denkmal deutscher Geschichte und Kunst* [Berlin: 1907]). *Quellenuntersuchungen, Texte zur Geschichte der heiligen Elisabeth* (*Neues Archiv der Gesellschaft fur ältere deutsche Geschichtskunde* [1909]). *Die Heilige Elisabeth und Papst Gregor IX* (Hochland: 1909).

Wildemann, Stephan, *Die heilige Elizabeth* (Karlsruhe: 1940).

INDEX